GODLY MEN MAKE GODLY FATHERS

BY 15 CHRISTIAN FATHERS

Doug Lauffer, Eduardo Quintana,
Mark Pudlowski, Clarke Lauffer,
Dave Lacine, Brian P. Swift,
Brian E. Panichelle, Paul Gray,
William Fawcett Jr., Dr. Ed Kropf,
Paul Dimtroff, Trevor N. Olsen,
Darcy Hawk and Ron Razete

Foreword by John Guest

Godly Men
Make Godly
Fathers

Godly Men Make Godly Fathers™
Copyright © 2017 by D.K. Lauffer,
Motivation Champs Publishing in The United States of America

Printed Version
ISBN- 978-09981194-4-1

978-09981194-4-1

Cover Picture by Adam Sherez, Sea of Galilee, Israel
Found at https://unsplash.com/ @mr_sherez
Beautiful, Free Photos, Gifted by the World's Most Generous Community of Photographers.

The book was printed in the United States of America.
To order additional copies of this book, contact:
Motivation Champs Publishing
http://motivationchamps.com/contact
Or, Doug Lauffer (412) 527-2213
You may also contact one of the book's authors whose contact information is at the end of each of their respective chapters.

Godly Men
Make Godly
Fathers

Foreword

By Rev. Dr. John Guest

Most of us "MEN" who claim to love the Lord Jesus, really struggle to be "authentic" followers of Christ. This, no less so, in being a dad to our children, and the spiritual leader in our homes.

It is a privilege to be a "Dad." To have a son or daughter who calls you "Dad." Just this year one of my daughters (my wife and I have four daughters) simply addressed an envelope to me, "My Dad!" I was so moved with all that it expressed. "My" Dad. I wasn't just "Dad" – I was her Dad. She called me "Her Dad!" When I read those two words, "My Dad" I was moved to tears! This, after all the years of being "Her Dad" - with all the ups and downs, the heartbreaks and joys, the successes and failures, the mundane and the momentous times! "My Dad" said so much more than just those two words.

The men who have authored the series of testimonials in this book share their hearts and bare their souls in so doing. Each one relays to us out of his very personal experience, 'diamond like' treasures for us who would be "Godly Fathers!" Added together, you hold in your hand as you read this collection of essays, a treasure trove of "day to day wealth," out of the lives of men just like you!

What each of these "Dads" hold in common is a deep sense of their relationship to their Heavenly Father. My Dad died when I was 7 years of age! He committed suicide. I remember the day when a policeman came to our home in Oxford, England, and told my mother that my Dad was dead! I remember another day, this time in London, England, when I was 18 years old. It was the day I handed my life over to the Lord Jesus as my Savior! It was at a "Billy Graham" meeting. The month was May, the year 1954. That evening I left the Arena where Billy Graham preached, knowing that I had a Heavenly Father, who had come into my life, and who would never

1

leave me. I was His Son and He was my Father. He gave me a sense of destiny for what my future held – both here on earth and when I died. Heaven was my ultimate Home, and God was my ultimate Father. Through surrendering to Christ at the Cross, my life took on a whole new direction with a whole new significance! That transformed the young man I was and the Father I would become!

One way or another, the men who author these chapters tell of their endeavor to be a Dad to their children, reflecting, not always self-consciously, that they have a Heavenly Father who cares for them and their children. These men want the very best for you as a Dad, as well as for your children.

I want to thank The Rev. Doug Lauffer for inviting these men to pass on to us the "Fatherhood Wisdom" from their years of experience. Doug, himself, has been the most amazing Father to his own children, as well as a dear friend of each of these men – including me! He is "authentic" — "The Real Deal!"

Doug knows the realness of our Heavenly Father making us a part of His Family. That when we invited the Lord Jesus to come into our lives, we became The Father's personal children: That His Spirit witnesses with our spirits that this is so real we can call Him "Abba" – "Dad" – "My Dad." So, we can go to Him, our Heavenly Father, and seek His help in being the Dad to our children that He calls us to be, and that we want to be! "Go For It!"

For as many as are led by the Spirit of God, they are the sons of God. For ye have not received the spirit of bondage again to fear; but ye have received the Spirit of adoption, whereby we cry, Abba, Father. The Spirit itself bears witness with our spirit, that we are the children of God: Romans 8:14-16

God Bless You,
John Guest

About John Guest

 Reverend Dr. John Guest was born and raised in Oxford, England. While training to become an engineer, he came to a personal relationship with Jesus Christ at a Billy Graham crusade in 1954. Following his graduation from Trinity College in Bristol, England in 1961, he was ordained in the Church of England. John also holds Honorary Doctorate degrees from Geneva College and Grove City College.

John came to the United States in 1966 to work for Scripture Union USA among high school and university students. In 1968, along with his bride Kathleen, John was called to Pittsburgh to work for the Pittsburgh Experiment – with a vision that Pittsburgh might become as famous for God as it was for steel.

As part of the vision for Pittsburgh, in 1970 John founded the Coalition for Christian Outreach, a ministry to university students; co-founded the Pittsburgh Leadership Foundation; Trinity Episcopal School of Ministry; and the South American Missionary Society.

Over the past twenty years, John has been invited to address major cities as a spokesman for the Christian faith throughout the United States and around the world, in such diverse nations as Ukraine, Russia, Uganda, Ghana, Cuba, Romania and Albania. In this role, he has spoken to nearly two million people. One by-product of this work was the formation of Church Planters International, and the planting of some 1,300 new churches in the former Soviet Union.

Dr. Guest served as Senior Rector of St. Stephen's Episcopal Church in Sewickley, PA for twenty years. He became the first

Senior Pastor and Rector of Christ Church at Grove Farm, a church plant in the northwest suburbs of Pittsburgh, PA, where he served for fifteen years. He also served as the Chaplain at the Ocean Reef Club in Key Largo, Florida for four years. Recently he returned to Christ Church at Grove Farm and serves as Minister at Large and speaks at church and community events when available.

For twenty years, John's sermon messages were heard on the LifeFocus with John Guest daily radio program in Western Pennsylvania. John was also a recording artist in the late 60's (part of the British invasion), and has authored more than a half dozen books.

Dedication and Preface

Each father who has written a chapter in this book, **Godly Men Make Godly Fathers** share many things in common. All of us would admit that WE ARE NOT PERFECT fathers! It is our prayer that by reading our book you will want to be a more godly person.

However, declaring that we are imperfect is NOT an excuse to not become better fathers and to admit when we are wrong is not an excuse for our faults. In our book you will read many inspirational and wondrous stories of our lives as fathers. As authors of this book, we all agree and believe that at least one of these chapters will bless you and may even CHANGE your life to become more and better as a parent, and a person.

We dedicate our book to all our mothers, fathers, teachers, coaches, caregivers and so many others who made and continue to make sacrifices — small and great for us. This is dedicated to you MOM, DAD et al! ☺

God is Great, so is Dad; Your ONLY Recipe is/was Love!
You taught us and showed us the following truth.

GODLY MEN MAKE GODLY FATHERS!

Thank you for your encouragement, discipline, inspiration and most of all, unconditional love.

In our book, there are many touching stories that prove how important dads are. So before you read our book, say a prayer and also consider the following facts. The facts are indeed alarming; please consider these statistics:

- Children in father-absent homes are almost four times more likely to be poor. In 2011, 12 percent of children in married-couple families were living in poverty, compared to 44 percent of children in mother-only families.
- 43% of US children live without their father
    - [US Department of Census] 2014

- 71% of pregnant teenagers lack a father.
    - [US Department of Health and Human Services press release, Friday, March 26, 1999]
- 71% of high school dropouts come from fatherless homes.
    - [National Principals Association Report on the State of High Schools]

- Even after ascertaining income levels, youths in father-absent households still have significantly higher odds of incarceration than those in mother-father families. Youths who never had a father in the household experienced the highest odds of incarceration.
    - [Harper, Cynthia C. and Sara S. McLanahan. "Father Absence and Youth Incarceration." Journal of Research on Adolescence 14 September 2004: 369-397]

Things have not changed very much in almost six (6) years. By the Grace of Almighty God, LET'S do something about it! The fathers of this book have messages of direction, hope and power for godliness. Not a form of godliness, a fake lifestyle but a lifestyle that is Christ-like.

Fathers need to live the kind of living that is a winsome! Lives that inspire us all to be more like Jesus. Christ-like godly dads should be able to win their own children to the Lord Jesus. Their examples and leadership should bring our families, friends, relatives and communities into the paths of peace and lives also can be filled with joy and peace that comes from knowing God!

For I am not ashamed of the gospel of Christ: for it is the power of God to salvation to everyone that believes… Romans 1:16.

Doug Lauffer, Summer 2017 Leetsdale, Pennsylvania, USA

Table of Contents

Godly Men
Make Godly
Fathers

My JOY Factor in Fatherhood

By Doug Lauffer

There are three (3) things that are of greatest importance and impact and my life; I call it my JOY Factor in Fatherhood.

1. Jesus
2. Others
3. You

Jesus came into my life in abundance and power when I was 17 years old. Up until that time, Jesus, to me was a religious figure in history. He was a great teacher and wonderful person but, He was not the Son of God nor was He anymore a Messiah than Mahatma Gandhi, Gautama Buddha/Siddhartha, Mohamed, The Dali Lama, Clara Barton or any other significant world-changing person of antiquity. This includes contemporary modernity.

In short, I had no core belief about Jesus being anything more than a Jewish carpenter who became a transformative religious leader.

But then, it happened! As I was reading the New Testament and particularly the Gospel of Mark, I became a believer. There were other factors that God used to open my heart and mind such as Christians that influence me but, it was while I had been reading what became to me, God's Word, The Bible, that I actually opened my heart to God, to Jesus.

From that time on, I considered myself a Christian. Before, I only attended church because my sweetheart, Vicki, went. Now, I loved God and wanted to be with His people at church, Bible studies, coffee houses—anywhere His people gather.

Jesus took first place and I began to grow in my faith and knowledge of Him. One way, I knew He had changed me was that I had a compelling feeling and desire to let other people know that Jesus saves! Jesus saves from what? Well, in the Bible I read where Jesus said that He came to seek and to save that which was lost. People are lost because of sin; for me I recognized my sin, I was a sinner. I knew how I needed to be more forgiving and kind toward others and that I really was not like that because of sin in my life.

What did the Gospel message mean to me? It meant that I was a lost sinner and needed salvation. Up to that time, I never even really thought about sin. I did not think that I was a bad person; I just did not think about my spiritual condition compared to what Jesus taught about my spiritual condition.

Whenever, I learned that Jesus "loves me", I also learned that He died for me on the cross for my sins. I had thought that Jesus was crucified because He disrupted the Jewish nation and Roman Empire in that part of the world. The Romans and Jewish leaders wanted Him brutally punished and killed for His capital offenses against "The Empire".

However, I learned from reading the New Testament in The Holy Bible that was not the case at all. Jesus came into the world to bring salvation and give us a way to transform our world with love and peace. Jesus taught us that God forgives and changes us and therefore, we can do the same. We can forgive others and change too by the Power of The Holy Spirit, the Spirit of the Living God.

All of this was proven to me by the resurrection of Jesus from the dead after he was killed, crucified and rose from the dead. I did not immediately understand what was happening to me but, I knew that Jesus came into my life and I was a different person.

By receiving Jesus Christ as my personal Lord and Savior, I was submitting to Him to the Lord, i.e. The Boss of my life, my Messiah, my Savior, my Lord and my God!

This was an amazing time in my life; I had no shame in talking about Jesus, I was proud to be following Him and promoting His message to others! Certainly not everybody was very receptive to my evangelistic zeal but, if somebody did not want to listen, I knew there were a thousand others that I could try to share Christ with them.

The Norwin High School was my mission field; I told everybody about Him, all of the students, teachers, staff and even the school's board members. Whenever I finished that mission, I asked Jesus if I could tell everybody in Irwin, Pennsylvania about Him and His love. I felt God say yes, GO and tell them!

People often would say to me, "Doug you know I go to church." I would reply, "It's not about church, it is all about Jesus and how He wants to have personal relationship with YOU!"

My life now was developing and continues to develop based on what I consider JOY, Jesus, Others and You.

An old song characterizes one of my daily practices. It's called, *Jesus and Others and You* written my by B. Metzger in 1951. Here are the lyrics.

Jesus and others and you

What a wonderful way to spell joy

Jesus and others and you

in the life of each girl and each boy

"J" is for Jesus for He has first place,

"O" is for others you meet face to face,

"Y" is for you, in whatever you do,

Put yourself third and spell JOY.

Jesus is first in my life; each day I ask him to lead, guide and direct my life. With Him first, I believe that He can help me and give me wisdom and guidance. I need direction for my life daily and who better than Jesus Christ to ask for direction. Often, I get an answer "from Jesus" that comes as a feeling deep down inside of me that I should to talk to somebody or I should read something to help me find answers and direction so that I can help others. And, there are actually other times, when He, I feel He is super-naturally guiding me.

Why do you try this? Right now, ask Jesus, yes right now to lead and help you. I believe that you will see at some point in your life, if not TODAY what I mean!

For my work in life, I have always asked Jesus to guide me. I am minister, a scientist, a professor, an inventor, an author and of course a Christian father. I have always asked the Lord Jesus to guide me and help me to be that best that I can be in all of my activities.

Jesus gives me JOY; I give myself JOY by following Him.

Others are second because I have learned this from the example Jesus gave us when he was living here on earth. Jesus put others before Himself on so many occasions. He would be sure that the hungry were fed and that the sick were taken care of or even healed. The focus of Jesus was on others!

Put others before me. I should consider others before me. For example, if there is only one sandwich on a plate, I always try to make sure others have the first chance to take it. If somebody does, I just say to myself, I may have wanted it but, by putting others first I am being like Jesus. And, I want to be like Jesus Christ. The word

Christian literally means, "a little Christ". I am Christ-like, a little Christ, when I am like Jesus.

Whenever I was a missionary in Senegal North West Africa, I knew I was there for others. My whole life was about others. We had a dispensary for the sick, a literacy program to teach people how to read; we worked on translating the Bible. It was really hard work but, I had JOY in my heart!

Whenever I had my company, Total Access Corporation, my products and services were for others. Our mission was to have the best products and services for our customers.

As a professor, my students come first before me. A self-described "muscular" Christian is how President Theodore Roosevelt, referred to himself and that these are the kind of Christians that he likes to meet. The muscle to me says, "People don't care what you know until they know how much you care!"

Jesus, Others and YOU, me, I should put myself last. This spells JOY and my life is literally filled with JOY.

Jesus said that I should love my neighbor as I love myself. Jesus said to owe nobody anything but love.

This kind of life in Jesus Christ as a youth and maturing man, gave me a peace and happiness that I never imagined I could experience. I have the delight and pleasure to see my own children come to believe and follow Jesus. They too are experiencing the elation and many times bliss of a life in Christ Jesus.

None of them are ordained reverends but all of them are ministers of Jesus by serving Him and others in their churches and communities.

YOU! Jesus others and me, by putting myself last, where God wants me to be, I have discovered that serving others is the path to JOY. I am the boss of me and I follow Jesus. You are the boss of you and you have to choose whom you will follow. You can follow any guru or philosophy of the world affords but, I am convinced that if you follow Jesus you will find the JOY that you seek. God's Word says, *"In His presence is fullness of JOY"!* See Psalm sixteen and verse eleven, 16:11.

My life became one of trying to inspire others. When asked, "Why do you live as you do?" I am always ready to give the reason, JESUS. He teaches me to serve and put OTHERS before me. It is written in God's Word; consider this, *"Always be prepared to give an answer to everyone who asks you to give the reason for the hope that you have. But do this with gentleness and respect."* Peter 3:15

This is my JOY Factor in Fatherhood. Do you have a factor that inspires your fatherhood, your life?

Are you living in the JOY of JESUS? Are you ready to live in JOY? Just ask Jesus to give you JOY; Jesus will thrill you as He delights to answer your prayers, indeed a JOYOUS wonder!

About Doug Lauffer

Doug is a minister, entrepreneur and a professor. Ordained in 1976, he has served churches in Pennsylvania, Sénégal and Uganda, Africa. Doug is a professor at Community College Beaver County, Monaca, Pennsylvania. Professor Lauffer teaches Information Technology and Philosophy.

His Master in Theology is from the University of Balamand, Lebanon's Saint John of Damascus School of Theology; his Master of Science is from the University of Pittsburgh in Telecommunications. He has a BA, Bachelor of Arts with a major in French and a BSBA, Bachelor of Science in Business Administration from Geneva College, Beaver Falls, Pennsylvania. Doug's Associate Degree is from Westmoreland County Community College, Youngwood, Pennsylvania. www.douglauffer.com

The Lauffers have four children and six grandchildren. Doug and Vicki Lauffer's third child was born in Simbandi Balant, Sénégal in Africa on December 19, 1978. They were pioneer missionaries there doing applied linguistics, cultural anthropology and translation work among the Manjak people. Their son, Brent Jacques FM Lauffer, was born in Africa. Brent was born as they later learned when Brent was 19 that he was born with a congenital liver disease, CHF, congenital hepatic fibrosis. He need a liver and kidney transplant and was listed in 2015. Brent was in management at Federal Express. He received a liver and a kidney transplants in January 2017 at The Cleveland Clinic Transplant Center. Brent Lauffer's fundraising website is at the following address. https://helphopelive.org/campaign/5201

Their other three children are married with children. Ken and Stephanie Lauffer have two daughters, Nadine and Tessa. Sharon and Rob Aho have two sons, Carson and Michael. Laraine and Matthew Furay have two sons, Elijah and Uriah.

Each of them are established in their chosen fields. All of the children are active in their communities and they also serve Jesus Christ in their churches as leaders and they serve the communities where they live.

Doug Lauffer's contact information is here below and he would welcome connecting with you or discussing what it is like to be living for the Lord Jesus!

douglaslauffer@gmail.com Phone: 412_527_2213
www.douglauffer.com
Twitter: @douglauffer
Facebook: Doug Lauffer and ProfessorDoug Lauffer
LinkedIn: www.linkedin.com/in/douglauffer
Doug is also on Google+, Pinterest, Instagram and Snapchat, Trip Advisor and etcetera.

The Manly Manual for Raising Kids

By Eduardo Quintana

It is true that it is easier for a father to have children than for children to have a real father. This became painfully obvious to me when my wife and I decided to adopt 3 wonderful boys.

I am a dad and I am also 49 years old! My wonderful wife (to whom I've been married for 25 beautiful years) and I started our family 6 years ago! I am the proud father of three energetic boys.

My 9-year-old is a soccer fan and has the skill to excel at it. He usually out-scores all the other players on both teams! He also loves basketball and has a real talent to sink that ball in the hoop. He is also very musically talented and plays the violin. He can play that violin like no other 9-year-old that I know. He is now learning a second instrument, the piano! He is truly a talented child!

I also have a 6-year-old that was born 9 weeks premature. He is a miracle baby because it is a miracle that he is alive! He was the first child we brought home but he is now the sandwich child too! He is strong willed and he is extremely smart! What a combination! When he was 4 he became obsessed with volcanoes and could tell you all about how the tectonic plates collide forming a magma chamber and that pushes the magma out through the surface, the earth's crust. Then, when it erupts, the pyroclastic flow travels at

17

400 miles an hour disintegrating everything in its path. After one year of volcanoes, he has finally moved on to other things and has a passion for building and creating things!

And then there is the baby of the family, our youngest who just turned 5 (five). Ever since he was born, he has had the most amazing smile. He can light up a room with his smile, his witty sense of humor and his tiny voice. He is extremely energetic and strong-willed, so he keeps mom and dad very busy from dawn to dusk. He is also musically talented. At three, he could repeat a tune he had just heard, note by note, using his voice.

"It is not flesh and blood but the heart
which makes us fathers and sons." - Friedrich Schiller

When most men my age are preparing to be empty-nesters and enjoy a quieter life (and more of their money too), my life is full of noise, activities, and expensive birthday parties! At an age when most men are getting to enjoy their grandchildren (for a little while and then turn them back over to their parents), I get to change diapers, go to PTA meetings, and get up in the middle of the night to comfort one of my boys! I get to spend my money on toys, violin classes and soccer leagues!

Please don't get me wrong. I am NOT complaining. I am just setting the scenario so you and I can have an earnest talk about what it means to be a dad. There may be several reasons why you grabbed this book; maybe curiosity got the best of you or you are seeking information because you are a new dad or grandfather. Perhaps you never had a father and now you want to be a good dad to that little baby you are rocking back and forth as you stumble through this book. How do I know? Because I was that man reading parenting books at 2:00 am while I rocked my son in my arms.

Why did I do that? Because children do not come with an instruction manual. Someone should tell you that before you have kids. I mean, if you go out and buy a fancy entertainment system with surround-sound, DVD, 3-D TV, smart TV, and all the bells and whistles, and then you find out that you don't have the instructions, you would probably miss a lot of the good features that the system has. If you're a guy, and if you're anything like me, you probably don't usually read the instructions but then, you find out that there's something you want to do and you can't seem to figure it out, so you pull out the instructions and find out how to do it.

Unfortunately, children don't come with an instruction manual, or do they? God knew what kids would be like, after all he designed them. And he knew that children would drive parents to the point where we would call out to God for help!

I heard an interesting story about a young child behavior specialist who frequently delivered a lecture called "The 10 Commandments for Parents." The gentleman got married and became a father. Soon after, the title of his lecture was altered to "10 Hints For Parents." When he had a second child, the lecture became "Some Suggestions For Parents." When a third child was born, the man stopped giving lectures. [Paul Lee Tan. Encyclopedia of 7,700 Illustrations. (Rockville: Maryland: Assurance Pub., 1979. # 635]

The truth is that when we don't have any children by ourselves, and we have a lot of opinions about how to raise them, we say things like, "my children will never do that!" And then, one day, we have egg all over our face, because our children do exactly that which we thought they would not do. I am no expert, I am just a father of three and I have walked a few steps into parenthood. So, let me first give you this important piece of advice.

God has designed you to be a dad. Don't be mom's assistant. There are many dads that take a backseat to parenting and let the mom be the One that does it all. First, that is not fair for your wife! She is already working harder that you ever have, sleeping less, and stressed more! When she married you, I am sure she thought that you were a manly man, a leader, a take charge kind of person. Don't change that just because you now have children. Fathers have tons of skills that they never use at home.

Don't tell me that you run a landscaping business or a restaurant, but you can't dress and feed a 4-year-old? Don't tell me that you are a chef and can't make food for your baby! Take it on! Spend time with your kids and have your own ideas about what they need. It won't take away your manhood; it will give it to you. I did that. I spent more time with my kids. And I found out that I'm a pretty bad father. I make a lot of mistakes and half the time I don't know what I'm doing. But my kids love me. Go figure!

I heard a story about two children who were heard discussing their parents. The first said, "I'm really worried. Dad slaves away at his job so that I have everything I need, so I'll be able to go to college someday. Mom works hard washing and ironing, cleaning up after me, taking care of me when I am sick, and driving me everywhere I want to go. They spend every day of their lives working for me. But I'm worried." His friend asked, "What have you got to worry about?" The first little guy replied, "I'm afraid they're going to try to escape someday."

James Dobson in his book *The Strong-Willed Child* said, "Child rearing is like baking a cake. You don't realize you have a disaster until it's too late." But success in both child rearing and cake baking is best achieved by following the instructions, so I would like to offer you:

"Instructions for Successful Parenting."

I cannot include in one chapter everything that dad's and parents in general should consider in order to be successful in parenting. However, I can tell you what the most important step in successful parenting is. Then, I will let you discover the rest of it on your own. Remember, you will find all the answers in God's word.

The First and most important step in Successful Parenting is the Recognition that Your Child is a Gift from God. If you are going to survive the challenges of parenting, you must remember that your child is a gift from God.

When they graduate kindergarten, they are a gift from God. When your baby cracks his first joke, and it genuinely makes you laugh, they are a gift from God. When they throw up all over you and bodily fluids ruin your Mustang interior, they are a gift! And when they misbehave and make life challenging, they are still a gift from God.

Psalm 127:3-5

"Behold, children are a heritage from the LORD, the fruit of the womb is a reward. (4) Like arrows in the hand of a warrior, so are the children of one's youth. (5) Happy is the man who has his quiver full of them; ..." (NKJV)

If you want to survive parenthood remember that your children are worth the struggle and are a gift from God even if they sometimes act like the devil.

Can you say that your kids are a gift from God? You know that they are, even when you are in the middle of an epic battle with them. This verse tells us that they are a reward. Sometimes they will seem to be more of a punishment then a reward. Have you ever said, "What have I done to deserve this?" Now, have you ever said this regarding your children? If you haven't, the time will come when you will. One day you will need to remember that God tells us that they are a reward. God instructs us to look at our children as though they were arrows in the hands of a warrior. A warrior! According to the Webster dictionary, a warrior is a person who fights in battles and is known for having courage and skill.

That is so interesting! I never thought of myself as a warrior, a weapon bearing, sword swinging person who fights in battles and has courage and skill! But that's what God says about me, so it must be!

It does not matter if you think you are a warrior or not. You are a warrior because that is what God is telling us we (dads) are. And our job is to point them at something and let them go. Just like a bow and arrow! And that is what parenting is all about. Pointing your children in the direction in which they will go, building their character, and launching them into the world. It doesn't matter if they are your biological children or adopted. You are called to be a dad. And being a dad is an awesome and humbling responsibility!

I want to encourage you to be a great father, a faithful husband, and a Godly man. God created man in his image and one of the attributes of God is that of a father. Always remember that we share one of God's most precious attributes. This is an amazing responsibility and one that we must not take lightly. As a dad, created in God's image, you are called to build a firm foundation of character and a positive relationship with your children.

So, how do fathers build a firm foundation of character and a positive relationship with their children? I am glad you asked! There are four things God wants you to remember if you are serious about being a father. Once you have accepted that your children are a gift from God, you will need to stay focused on these four things. Are you ready?

First, always remember this verse. Write it down where you can see it daily. *"... a gentle tongue can break a bone"* (Proverbs 25:15)

In other words – there is great strength in gentleness. Do you show the same courtesy towards your kids that you expect from them? Can you praise your kids without adding anything negative – like, "Great job with the dishes tonight – pity your room's such a mess?" How about your discipline – is it firm and loving – or just firm? Do you discipline your children in front of others or do you respect them and love them enough to discipline them privately? Do you hug your kids regularly (If you don't they will find someone who will!!) Are you quick to go to their aid when there's a genuine need?

Your words and acts of loving-kindness today will build confidence in your sons and daughters. They will have the confidence to attempt anything if they know your love, acceptance, and gentle protection of them is assured no matter what.

Second, don't forget to Laugh! When was the last time you laughed with your children - instead of at them?

I recall this story in the bible of a man that was all alone; he had neither son nor brother. There was no end to his toil, yet his eyes were not content with his wealth. *"For whom am I toiling," he asked, "and why am I depriving myself of enjoyment?" This too is meaningless-- a miserable business!* (Ecclesiastes 4:8)

Dad's if you're always working, always disciplining, always giving orders and always serious – then your kids are missing out on something very important. And you may well be missing the enjoyment of watching your kids grow up – and so you may end up a very lonely man.

Playtime is a big part of being a child and unless you can get into it, you're being cut right out of a huge part of your child's life. Play sports with them. Discover which leisure things you like to do together and get into it.

Third, please remember that your kids are always learning.

It's no secret that most teachers – at least at Primary school level – are women. And for the most part I'm sure they're doing a fantastic job. But even our Education Department recognizes that more men are needed as teachers in our primary schools. What does this tell us? It tells us that it's best for children to get a balanced learning input from both mom and dad. (It's not always possible – but it's best).

And the single most important lesson a father can teach his child – is why they are alive. Listen to these words from Ephesians chapter 6 and verse 4.

Fathers, do not exasperate your children; instead, bring them up in the training and instruction of the Lord (Eph 6:4).

A father that teaches his child to follow the Lord will save them from living the frustration of a wasted life.

Train a child in the way he should go, and when he is old he will not turn from it (Proverbs 22:6).

My friend, you and your wife can teach your kids how things should work - - or you can abdicate your responsibility and let your kids learn about life from their friends, the TV/internet, and schools (That's a frightening thought).

Fourth, the last thing I want you to remember is to listen!

My dear brothers, take note of this: Everyone should be quick to listen, slow to speak and slow to become angry (This quote is from the Epistle of James chapter 1 and verse 19.)

When words are many, sin is not absent, but he who holds his tongue is wise (Proverbs 10:19).

So often dads just want to be dispensers of information. But if that's all communication is for you, then you have some extremely needy children. Especially if you have daughters, but sons are not much different in this department. Communication is about building a relationship – not just spewing out information.

And if you won't listen to your sons or daughters, then they will keep searching until they find someone who will! Wouldn't you much rather be that person? It's a tough job being a dad (or a mom for that matter). But you don't have to do it on your own!

For the eyes of the LORD range throughout the earth to strengthen those whose hearts are fully committed to him. (2 Chronicles 16:9a)

If you are His - - then He is yours! Don't complain that God is absent and not concerned about your life and plight as a Dad if you have never given Him the time of day. Never forget, if you are His, then He is yours - and He desires to make you the dad He created you to be.

To the fatherless/husbandless; To the emotionally abandoned; To those dads without a good fatherly example to follow, the Lord is.... A father to the fatherless, a defender of widows, is God in his holy dwelling. God sets the lonely in families (Psalm 68:5-6)

About Eduardo Quintana

Eduardo Quintana is the creator and founder of Manly Training Ministries. An organization designed to bring men to Christ and honor biblical manliness. You can visit Manly Training at https://manlytraining.com/ and subscribe to the blog and to the weekly newsletter. You can also hear Eduardo's message at The Manly Training Podcast on Soundcloud or iTunes:

iTunes: https://itunes.apple.com/us/podcast/manly-training-podcast/id1144341414?mt=2
Soundcloud: https://soundcloud.com/user-796716705

My testimony: Eduardo Quintana

I am a first-generation Christian. And by the grace of God, I am who I am today. It wasn't always that way. My life was a mess as far back as I can remember. My parents were divorced when I was a baby. My mother is a strong woman who did a great job raising me and teaching me right from wrong!

But our existence seemed to be marked by trouble. Hardship lurked around every corner. I had spent my childhood moving from place to place, many times without even saying good bye to my friends. My heart had started to get jaded! A lot of things happened to me in 1985 and 1986! I witnessed the horror of a natural disaster unlike any other, an 8.1 magnitude earthquake that shook Mexico City and killed hundreds of thousands of men, women, and children!

And, I was there, I saw apartment buildings pancaked and then saw the bodies of so many people! So many bodies that the stadiums were being used as morgues! In the middle of all of this, my girlfriend broke up with me, my dog was run over by a car and died and to top it off, in January of 1886 my biological father, whom I had just met 3 years prior, passed away of a massive heart attack!

These things took me to a very dark place in my life. But God had mercy on me and He saved me in a spectacular way. God led me to my own personal "Road to Damascus" and in September of 1986 I finally gave my life to my Lord Jesus Christ. I must confess that I never found God, God found me! He plucked me out of the pit of hell and placed me in his loving arms like a father does to a son when he is hurt. And this is how an 18-year-old boy was saved and how I became the man I am today. The very day I was saved, I told God I would serve him and I have never looked back.

Godly Men
Make Godly
Fathers

PAINFUL JOY

By Mark Pudlowski

Bolesny Radosc, Polish for "My Experience"

May 11th, 2002, my two youngest children were just given a harsh reminder from their father to put their shoes on so we could go celebrate my friend's birthday with his family, and then the phone rang. Mr. Pudlowski the caller said? I asked who is calling; his voice was somewhat hesitant to respond. He then began to tell me that he is the senior pastor at a church in Gulfport Mississippi and that he had terrible news for me and my family. He began his next few words with distance and grief. He explained that my oldest son Joseph John Pudlowski had gone home to be with the Lord through a tragic accidental drowning. Time stood still! I can't begin to tell you how deeply my heart felt. This is just a dream I said…this isn't really happening…WAKE UP MARK, WAKE UP.

I went to the living room fell to my knees in front of my wife and children and began to cry out for us to join arms and just listen. Daddy has something to say that is going to change the rest of our lives. Joey is dead; he died in a tragic accident while serving the Lord in Mississippi on a youth disciple mission's trip and is now home with the Lord. Daddy was told that a current drug our Joey to the bottom of a bayou and held him there for fifteen minutes, and then God took him home. My life and family wasn't prepared for

29

this. You see my son just left my side, after spending 4 days at the men's retreat praying and sculpting our adult relationship for 80 solid hours. The last thing we did together at the retreat was him gently tucking me into bed, and attaching leg harness pillows between my crippled hips. Joey then told me he wanted me to listen to a song that God placed on his heart, "I Can Only Imagine" by Mercy Me. I told him it was a very nice song and kindly thanked him for sharing it with me. I didn't know why my son wanted me to listen to what heaven was going to be like when we arrive, but in retrospect Joey was giving me insight to an experience he was moving towards without knowing its meaning. From that day forward, each and every time I hear that song I am reminded how precious life is. When I sing along I change one verse that say's *"when that day comes and I find myself standing in the sun"*, to when that day comes and I find myself standing with my son. One day that stanza will come to fruition, and yet I can only imagine what real heaven will be like.

My son was laid out in the funeral home just one block from my home. My family and I waited 2 days for his lifeless body to be shipped back home, with full military honor guard. I went to the funeral home at midnight to greet his body being delivered, but to my surprise I encountered a prayer warrior from my church doing the exact same thing, waiting on Joey. She kindly told me that I didn't need to be there and that God woke her from her sleep to assume the position of the gate keeper and to protect my spirit from grieving. I didn't understand why, nor was I about to question God about anything at this point, since he also provided nine (9) man U.S. Navy Honor Guard surrounding my son. So I went home and wept. God is so good!

When my wife and I had to identify his body, the words from my wife solved so many questions. She told me "just remember, it's only his shell, **Joey is HOME!** In spite of the pain it made perfect sense. So I look forward standing with my son, just like the song

30

say's. But now the detours of life starts. This side of heaven I will never understand unless I use God's word to comfort our pain. Isaiah 40:28-31 was my son's favorite verse; *Hast thou not known? hast thou not heard, that the everlasting God, the LORD, the Creator of the ends of the earth, fainteth not, neither is weary? There is no searching of his understanding. He giveth power to the faint; and to them that have no might he increaseth strength. Even the youths shall faint and be weary, and the young men shall utterly fall: But they that wait upon the LORD shall renew their strength; they shall mount up with wings as eagles; they shall run, and not be weary; and they shall walk, and not faint.* I'm in complete awe that this verse being so many times used in dialogue with other parents who have also experienced the death of a child.

The day my son died, communication using email and the internet was new to me. Joey and I began emailing one another and I liked it a lot. He was following in his father's footsteps in the United States Navy, but when this happened I sat in front of the computer and sent him just one last email. Joey did you suffer? Were you in pain? Were you afraid? Did you cry out for your mother and father? Then I paced back and forth knowing that if I pressed the send button, this email will ALWAYS go unanswered. Twenty minutes later I pressed the send button and waited for a supernatural response. Just a simple yes, thumbs up, or even a wink, but nothing happened. I must have looked for a response for the next few days and then a friend of mine, my choir director, my pastor, my brother in Christ grabbed me away from the crowd of grieving people at my house and looked at me smiling and said these words I will never forget; "Can you imagine what it must have been like for your son to fall asleep in the water and to wake up in the arms of Christ"! There was my answer....I never looked again, so now I move forward, but how?

The next year wasn't any easier for me and my family. They say time heals all wounds, that's a myth, time just makes the wounds older, and for the next 12 months I lost a father-in-law, an uncle, a step-father, a grandfather, a grandmother, an aunt, and two childhood friends. My friends asked me if I was shooting for the Job award by spending more time in funeral homes and gravesites. Funny thing about comments about death, none of them make any sense if you think of it; like "they look at peace" or "they did a wonderful job on the body" or even this one which I could never figure out, "how are you doing?" When you bury a child you aren't doing…you just are. Everybody else moves on after the funeral, your life just moves, and most of us with this experience still struggle.

I would like everyone who reads this to be reminded that my children, my wife, my ministry, my home and all that God has me responsible for must be held with a loose grip because it doesn't belong to me. That's how I grieved my sorrow, by thanking God for the 18 years I had been blessed with my son, and if in fact my son had the opportunity to return for one second to look at his Daddy, he would refrain because of being with his Heavenly Father is so much better, but I'm selfish and look forward to that day of seeing Christ face to face, as my son gives me the tour of the Kingdom. It's just like my son, to beat me to Heaven as I was to greet him there! Can't wait to hug that boy!

To bury a child isn't a group people will stand in line to join. You can't be invited into this group. It's a special group with special people in it. Father's Day, Mother's Day, and the anniversary dates i.e. birthdays, death dates are sometimes just as painful as the event itself. But if you happen to be blessed by being a member of this group, welcome aboard and remember that God the Father is the leader of this group, as He also experienced the temporal death of His Son Jesus Christ because of times like this! I believe that when we cry God catches our tears and waters the flowers in Heaven with them. Scripture say's there will be no more pain or crying tears in Heaven, which is why we cry ABBA here and now. Take the time to eliminate a lot of worry from future events by knowing there isn't anything you can do to prevent death…Nothing! Scripture reminds us that there is an appointed time for ALL of us to die; Hebrews 9:27 *"And as it is appointed unto men once to die, but after this the judgment"*:

So, parent remember this, to avoid the White throne judgment, where the finality of one's life is eternally cast into the lake of fire and destruction, teach them to know what is and to prepare for the Bema seat of judgment and the Bema seat Judge and His LOVE that saves you.

So why do I call this section "Painful Joy"? Simply put it is the carnal certainty and brevity of life which contributes to the pain…vs. the Eternal life in Christ we can begin to experience right now. The Joy of the Lord isn't something you have to wait for! Even in the current pain we experience can be purified through His Joy, His Purpose, His Love, His loving arms to wake up in. This promise of Hope in Jesus Christ is available immediately. The shortest distance to the cross is about 11 inches, starting with your mind and ending at your heart.

About Mark Pudlowski

Mark Pudlowski is a 59 year old happily married man of 30 years to Susan L. Pudlowski, sons Joseph John Pudlowski (Home with the Lord May 11th 2002), Ryan Adam Pudlowski and Daniel Phillip Pudlowski, and Clyde the wonder dog (11 yr. old Basset hound and treatment partner in ministry).

Mark is the Founder and Chief Counsel at the Family of God Biblical Reasoning Prayer Center, 1133 Lincoln Way, White Oak, Pennsylvania 15131. Mark's education all started in the United States Navy as a Surface Warfare Specialist, Boatswains mate 2nd class, then retiring in 1994. He pursued a Masters' degree in Social Work and Psychology. Upon graduation Mark underwent bi-lateral hip replacement and began a career in the field of Family Treatment therapist.

Mark was called by our Lord to take on the role as Chief Operations Officer of the Domestic Abuse Counseling Center, the largest platform of batterer's intervention/Anger Management this side of the Mississippi.

During his 15 year tenure with DACC, Mark was also the program director at the Allegheny County Jail Anger Management/Domestic Violence intervention unit. During his time with DACC the Holy Spirit prompted a career change as God would have his work move away from secular counseling to Biblical Reasoning utilizing the WORD of God as the benchmark and final authority of serving the populations surrounding his ministry. Mark does not charge a fee for his services, but willingly accepts love offerings and donations and states there isn't a place in scripture that allows me to help my fellow man and charge a fee for answering the call of the LORD. One reason I struggled by answering the call of God was the decision to walk away from a $85,000.00 a year job, working only 25 hours a week to a ministry with ZERO salary. I knew that God desired ALL of my time to focus on HIM… HIS WORD… and HIS people who needed help. So for the last almost two (2) years God has directed and validated each and every moment within the ministry and my social circles. Mark is an accomplished author with his first book, *Taking Back The Rainbow – Returning the family to the family of God.* His life passions are glorifying God, serving Him alone by serving others and his family and friends. Most important is his love for the WORD and his desire to remain obedient to the ministry and vision God has placed in his heart. Favorite Scripture verse 2 Chronicles 7:14 King James Bible.

2 Chronicles 7:14 *If my people, who are called by my name, will humble themselves and pray and seek my face and turn from their wicked ways, then I will hear from heaven, and I will forgive their sin and will heal their land.*

Godly Men
Make Godly
Fathers

The Journey Being a Dad

By Clarke Lauffer

When I first became a father some 43 years ago it was something I wasn't prepared for. When you are young and get married the logical thing to do is begin a family.

Even though, you most likely have just left your own family with some dysfunctional issues. I mean, just being a member of a family does not mean that you know about raising a family.

So here you are as a 20 year old not far from being a kid yourself planning to have a kid. We had our first daughter and she was amazing. A beautiful little bundle of joy. We called her Melanie Joy. So here we are as a very young couple learning the stages of parenting. Some years were great and other years were awful. What we discovered is parenting is not easy and many times not very fun.

A few years later we had our second daughter Jessica. She too was a beautiful little free spirit. So here I was a man outnumbered by three girls, you can't win!

What did I learn as these girls lived with us for around 19 years? I learned that being a Father requires great wisdom and grace from our Heavenly Father. God the Father has perfect skill in knowing how to love, guide, discipline and restore. He alone knows how to guide a heart in the ways of life that can prevent a life from being destroyed. It took many years for me to learn how to be a healthy father and I'm still learning new things from My Heavenly Father. What is wonderful is now we have 6 grandchildren, ages 12 and under. This is where we get to use the skills and wisdom we received throughout all these years. Sometimes you hear people say I wish I knew back then what I know now. Well, that is the case with being a Dad. Not only in child rearing skills but every aspect of life. It takes a lifetime if were open to humbling ourselves to learn how God Fathers each of us. He is so merciful, patient, kind, gentle, and never condemning.

The Bible talks about a supernatural power that is available for daily living. This power comes from God the Holy Spirit who actually lives within the Christian. Every resource we humanly need to be effective Fathers comes from the Holy Spirit. The key, ARE WE WILLING to yield and listen to His counsel for Fatherhood?

What happens to many of us Dads is we get overwhelmed, inpatient, frustrated, and just stressed out. We try to find outlets to actually escape the family. We work longer, play sports or develop hobbies to burn time. All the while our kids are begging us for attention, they just want to play and hang out with us. Yet we are blinded to this privilege of being needed as a Dad who loves to be with their kids. Many of those who are reading this book realize we missed many hours of being a dad because of our "disconnect".

Yet many of you are in the midst of the prime years of raising your kids. Do you know that you have the time to slow down the clock and be with your kids?

I remember having my face in the paper as they waited patiently for me to pay attention to them.

How I would give anything to go back in time, cancel the paper, get off my duff and go play with them.

There is no greater joy in being a godly father than, pouring who God made you to be, into the hearts and lives of your children.

Their depth of understanding about what makes a rich and full life of meaning comes from those who taught us so many fascinating things about living life. Your experiences are really something your children will absorb and make part of their own lives.

If you want them to love, know and follow the Lord, they will if you let them know who He has become to you.

Sharing the scripture, praying with them, pointing things out in Creation to their little eyes will make them see the world from a Biblical perspective and they will always marvel at how great our God is! Allow yourself to be vulnerable around your children and teach them how much you depend upon God for everything in your life. This example will teach them to learn about faith and in their lives they will trust in the Lord.

Here are some things to think about as a Dad no matter how old your kids are;

1. Do they always know your available and care?

2. Do you listen and speak truth into their lives?

3. Do you take time to just hang out and have fun together?

4. Do you respect their decisions; counsel them if a better alternative may be advisable?

5. Are you enthusiastic when they succeed?

6. Will you be willing to rescue them what they are in trouble?

7. Will you make up for lost time by spending time with their kids, your grandkids?

8. Will you leave a legacy of love and faith toward God they will always remember?

Always be available to just listen when your kids need to talk. Even when the conversation seems not very important, when you patiently listen, it will build in their hearts an openness to talk when it's critically important.

39

As you listen to them be prepared to bring Godly counsel from God's Word when they are not thinking from a Christian point of view. Try to see things from their vantage point before you bring your perspective, Biblical point of view.

Spend time on weekends as a family, have meals together, play games and sports, take vacations as an extended family with Great Grandparents too. Sometimes just meet for coffee or stop by their house when they are grown up with their own family. Each time spent together builds relationship and memories.

Realize that they will sometimes make decisions that are not the best; however, respect their opinions and choices so they will always want to get your opinion and wisdom. This is most important in case they are open to changing their mind. If they don't change their mind, still be supportive unless it goes against the truth and will of God's Word. Then, you will need to be assertive.

Children love to call or stop by when they have a big win in their life, they know you are their biggest fan and there is nobody more important than Dad when it comes to sharing their personal success. Always be thrilled and excited about anything that they share that has been a major accomplishment.

When times of crisis come do whatever you can to soften the blow and lighten the burden of their cares and heartaches. Our kids when they were little always ran to us for comfort and they will never stop coming even when they are older. They have the desire to be in family as long as you live, you are still family.

Kids, they have a God-inspired desire to be a part of family. They know, as long as dad is around, you can be depended upon to find a solution for whatever is currently overwhelming them.

All Dads have regrets but there is a wonderful way to make it up to your kids. Spend time being a Grandad with your grandkids. I remember the first time we went to the Jersey Shore with our first grandson. I went back in time in my mind as I built sandcastles with our little Logan. My daughter made a collage of us playing on the beach together that hangs in my office. I look at this many times and in wonder think about how fast life moves. I remember, like it was yesterday, as my daughter Melanie watched me play with her son, she also went back in time in her heart remembering us together on that same beach. I now have that same privilege playing with her second son little Gabriel. It is not a slight thing when they who are so fresh from God love us. This holds true to my daughter Jessica as she many times has been with us at the Jersey Shore as I play with Isabella, Mia, Lilianna and now little Elias Clarke aka Bubba. The pictures, memories and all the years we have enjoyed just playing together is the best part of being a Dad!

Last but certainly not least is the personal legacy you build as a Father who listens and Prays with his kids, to this day I pray with my daughters when life is very hard.

They know, even though I'm far from being perfect, that my trust is in God our Heavenly Father who truly is the perfect loving Father; Whom we all need. As they have seen my faith never waver in the worst of times, it anchors them in the reality that our God can be trusted completely to get us through whatever we may face in life.

The last 21 plus years of being a Dad has been spent serving as a pastor pointing others to the God of all hope the God of all comfort. I leave you with this; get to know the Lord; and as you know Him more intimately, His life will flow through you to your kids leaving behind a legacy of perfect love for all eternity!

Special Thanks to my beloved brother, Doug, who challenged me to write on my experiences being a father which has truly been a blessing just remembering I'm still a Father.

"For this reason I bow my knees before the Father, from whom every family in heaven and on earth derives its name, that He would grant you, according to the riches of His glory, to be strengthened

with power through His Spirit in the inner man, so that Christ may dwell in your hearts through faith; and that you, being rooted and grounded in love..." St. Paul's Epistle to The Ephesians 3:14 to 17

About Clarke Lauffer

Clarke is pictured here with his wife, Cindy. They have been married 46 years. They are also shown here with their grandchildren

We planted Calvary Chapel Westmoreland back in March of 1996 with just a few families. We met in a YWCA for the first 12 years and were blessed to buy the current location in 2008. We were away from this area for about 15 years while we lived outside of Philadelphia. While there we were part of various Bible teaching fellowships but didn't really find home until we began to go to Calvary Chapel of Philadelphia. While there, we really began to grow and return back to our first love, Jesus.

We sold our beautiful church building in January of 2017 we had been in since 2008. To move Calvary Chapel into the Greensburg Shopping Center on Pittsburg Street in Greensburg Pa. The new location makes us more accessible to the center of the city with unlimited parking and handicap accessibility.

The simple laid back style and verse-by-verse teaching throughout the Bible got our spiritual attention. Also, the Worship of God was so real and heart stirring that our hearts began to soften.

We had started out when we first got married to be missionaries with New Tribes Mission reaching those who never once heard of Christ. After Bible College it became apparent that I wasn't suited for that kind of life, as I have no brains in my hands and missionaries to survive have to do many mechanical things on the mission field. We always had a sense of God's call on our lives, but lost the vision and got stuck in the world of self-indulgence.

Currently, I am a bi-vocational pastor and work as a sales rep for an Optical Wholesaler. My wife Cindy is an administrative secretary for the church and also a full-time grandmother to our 6 priceless grandchildren.

We know God desires to do a work in every city of the world. We see by His hand of blessing and grace that He has chosen the people of this local Calvary Chapel to impact the world for His glory and honor. We love serving the Lord together and are so encouraged seeing people from all walks of life follow Jesus as His disciples.

Calvary Chapel Westmoreland County has a local radio station, Grace FM, Jesus The Living Water 100.3 broadcast over the Internet 24 / 7 / 365.

You can listen on-line at this link! http://www.graceradio.fm/

How did we get into a radio ministry? It all started with a prayer and a vision over 15 years ago... "What if we had true Biblical teaching 24 hours a day, 7 days a week?"

Jump ahead to today and that is exactly what you have: online bible teaching/sermons/preaching and Bible teaching on the radio and the World Wide Web, The Internet.

Please have a listen. Tune-in to 100.3 FM Greensburg, Westmoreland County, Pennsylvania area or listen LIVE online!

The Imbedded Thread

By Dave Lacine

So there we were, saying one last prayer together, fighting back tears as we sent one of our teenage sons off to find recovery from an addiction. We knew we could do no more than to "let go and release him" into God's hands as he ventured out. We remember well the conversation that we might not see him again. But we knew one thing. God could use anything, even heartbreak. We needed to be prepared to let go and trust all things to God, including our children. This story is one of a number of stories that could have its own chapter of God's Providential hand that is an imbedded thread in the tapestry of our family. For God once again restored, comforted, and healed as He has throughout our life.

What a daunting task to write about Fatherhood. My first reaction was to take a pass. After all, aren't there many others more qualified to write on this subject with years of research behind them who have a better grip on the subject? Of course there are. But everyone has their story and experience to share. And every story is unique and yet the same.

Background

I have two adult sons, four grandchildren, and a wonderful daughter in law, whom I prefer to call a daughter ever since she married our oldest son fourteen years ago. And most significantly, I have an amazing wife who has been and is my co-journeyer for the past 40 plus years.

I was raised in a Christian home with three brothers. I spent thirty four years in the insurance industry after college. The last seven, I completely shifted and left the familiar ground to pursue a call working with Christian Business Owners. But more than that I am a husband and a father which is where ministry begins - in the home.

Both of our sons are wired differently as we all are. One is a pastor and the other in business. But that is what they do, and of course they are so much more than that. We can mistakenly identify who we are with what we do. I am so grateful to have a meaningful relationship with both. We enjoy spending time together as adults. Of course, we have bumps on the road, differences of opinion, and conflicts that arise. However, we love to be together and share our lives with one another. And those differences, which sometimes bring conflict can teach us and bring us to greater understanding.

Love your children by loving your wife

I wish I could proudly say I have done a masterful job with this. I have not. Over our forty plus years of marriage we have had our rough patches to the point of separation, counseling, and wondering if we were going to make it. But God kept us close, even when we resisted! Through all of this, we have experienced God's Grace, a strong restored marriage, and have become the best of friends. There is no one I would rather spend time with. Through these difficulties, one thing that our children have seen over time is our commitment and determination to hang in there, even if only holding on to that imbedded thread at times. The best thing that parents can do is to love each other and the best thing I can do is to love my wife as an example to our children. So if you are reading this and are on shaky ground, hang in there! Sometimes that is all we can do to see it through the storms. But also remember to get help when you need it. We are so grateful for the help we received which brought us into the joy and beauty of forgiveness and restoration. And God is the One who can restore all things.

Ready or Not, Here They Come!

I have heard couples say that they are going to wait to have children until they are ready, financially set, and prepared. If that was the case, I would still be waiting. Are we truly ever prepared to be a parent, to be a father? My answer for this and so many other things is absolutely not. I am not prepared. But God equips us if we are only available and willing. And it may start with a prayer for our hearts to become available and willing. This is a process of lifelong learning. As life brings changes and our children grow, we need to change and our role as a father changes. At age 2, my children need a certain kind of instruction and safeguards. In the teenage years, it becomes a delicate balance as our children learn to navigate in making more decisions on their own. At age 30 or 35, perhaps what is most needed is a listening ear, encouragement, and affirmation. And more than providing answers, it may be the questions that are the most valuable.

We are Called by Name and are not the Same

What do I mean by this? As parents and as a father, we are given a great responsibility and stewardship. This is a gift from God. They are not really ours. They are given to us by God to nurture, encourage, and help them discover who they are and what they are made for. They are God's, created in His image and for His purpose. There is a Bible verse that talks about this: *"For we are God's handiwork, created in Christ Jesus to do good works, which God prepared in advance for us to do."* (Ephesians 2:10) Listen and Observe. Study your children, even at an early age. What are their tendencies? Persistent? Quiet? Determined? Artistic? Energetic? It's amazing what can be observed in children even at an early age. Be proactive in how to engage with them. Set the tone early in life that you may be able to carry it out in later years. There is a scripture that states: *Train up a child in the way he should go; even when he is old he will not depart from it.* (Proverbs 22:6). Be careful about letting a child go their own way when training and raising them, BUT we have a responsibility to teach, train, and encourage our children in the Greater Purposes of life which points to a relationship with Christ. Again, this can serve as a reminder to watch our children carefully for how they are wired. What are their gifts? Where do they need encouragement? Am I training one to be good in sports, when he is really a musician, or an artist? Make sure that we train them, and encourage them in the ways that God has made and created them to be.

Remove the Snooze Alarm

Some will say quality time is the most important. But can you have quality time without quantity time? You don't know when your child is going to want to talk or share about something of importance. Having quantity time provides the opportunity for quality experience. It's not just making the time for an event but a consistent occurrence. I remember, particularly when our children were in high school, I looked forward to driving them even a short distance to school, because I would never know when there would be an opportunity for a meaningful conversation and could never predict it. So look for ways to connect. What are the things your child likes to do? Then do it with them when you can and if it is physically possible. And if not, look for other things you can do in common together. The time together is what can produce the quality time.

They Are Watching

Do I practice what I Preach? Do I send the kids off to church but not attend myself? Am I kind to strangers? Do I display humility and apologize when I am wrong? Do I forgive? Do I keep my language and temper under control? We can talk about these things, but are we living them? None of us will be perfect, but when I miss a step am I willing to admit it and humbly make things right? Example is perhaps the most underestimated and can have a tremendous impact both on a positive side and a negative side. I am painfully reminded at times that this is a lifelong process. There is always room for improvement and for God's hand of refinement to take place in our lives.

Have a Family Mission Statement

This is one of those things I am clearer on now as an empty nester, but it would be well worth doing as your children are in the house. My wife and I have a simple mission statement which is: "To Draw Others Closer to God" This may mean something as simple as giving someone a cup of cold water when they need it, or as deep as journeying with someone over a season to help them through a crisis. This can also be an arbiter as we make family decisions and review our day. How helpful and insightful to have a family mission statement where at the end of the day you can all pause and reflect as well as be reminded of your family's mission.

Patience is a Lifelong tool along with the required Wisdom

Where would any of us be without patience? In the often quoted scripture verse in 1 Corinthians 13, read at many weddings on the subject of love, "Love is Patient". A definition of patience is long suffering. As our children grow up towards adulthood, and even afterwards, they are going to make decisions and mistakes, just as we have. Patience and Wisdom are required. When do we listen? When are we to speak into their lives? Certainly, as young children it is more about training and instruction, but as they grow older, do we shift from being the one who sets the boundaries to the one who is offering a listening ear? In the story of the Prodigal Son found in the Bible, it is interesting to see that even though a son left the home and spent the inheritance unwisely, the Father kept watching and

49

waiting patiently, and embraced his son and celebrated when he returned. If our heavenly Father is like this to us (and we are all prodigals at one time or another), shouldn't we be reminded of this and do the same? As I reflect on this, I am reminded of what a spiritual mentor once told me about people coming to faith in Christ. When the angels appeared to the Shepherds, they immediately responded and went to see the Christ Child. But then there were the wise men from afar who needed to take a long circuitous journey to seek and find the Christ. Everyone's journey to faith can be under different circumstances and timetables. Do we trust that God is in charge and will direct in these matters?

Stay away from the formulas

I am not talking about baby formula here. I am talking about if I do A and B, my child will do C. Some parents may seem to do everything right and the children can be a handful. Others may stop, start, make mistakes, and the kids turn out well. How do you explain this? I think it is a reminder that it's about grace. The grace of God is so essential for any of us to accomplish anything. How is it that one child is born into a difficult circumstance and another into a beautiful situation? There is so much we cannot control in terms of original environment: economics, opportunities, family, siblings, etc., and this should be a reminder to all of us that God is Sovereign and in the end, it is about relinquishing all to Him. After all, is not God desiring to be the ultimate Father of us all? Without His help, can we really accomplish anything? We take credit for much when it is really the grace of God and not about our tremendous abilities or talents or lack thereof.

Dedication

From the day our children were born, we dedicated them to the Lord. We knew we were ill equipped for such a responsibility. Whatever stage your children are at, dedicate them to the Lord for His greater purposes. Can you think of anything better to do than to commit your children to the Lord that they might be all that God has purposed them to be? I know this has been a great relief and reminder for us at times as we watch our children journey through difficult and unforeseen challenges. We cannot be there all the time for our children, but God can be!

Keep Legacy in Mind

Our relationship does not stop just because our children become adults. It continues. There are potentially grandchildren and other God given relationships to mentor, impart and interact with. To quote a mentor who stated to me what my mission was with our grandchildren: spoil them! In other words, show them through unconditional love and acceptance that they are the most special people in the world. We can be a comforting and safe place for them to go to when they know we love them just as they are. And remember, extravagant love and spoiling is not about things but can be a hug, a kiss, a high five, a thumbs up, or even the infamous tickle treatment!

Remember, our Children need their story too!

God is forming and shaping a story in all of us. Any good story often encounters peaks and valleys, good things and bad and are often the turning points that lead us to a personal relationship with God.   We need to navigate in all those things so that God can form His story in all of us, including our children.

The impact of Spiritual Practices

Spiritual Practices can start early and may not be what we think. One practice is saying grace before meals consistently where the family prays together. Another may be reviewing the highs and lows of the day with the family at dinner or when you are together. Where did we sense God's goodness or His presence? What was a difficult part of the day where we felt far from that? Having a rhythm of daily quiet time and spending time in the scriptures can be so necessary when family responsibilities can overwhelm. Filling your own tank in this manner can bring greater wisdom. Start with the New Testament Gospels and Proverbs if you do not know where to begin. Even a chapter a day can start you on a journey that will reap tremendous dividends for you as a father as you increase the potential for a closer walk with God.

How can we possibly make it?

In the end, for me, the foundation for Fatherhood has been the example of our Heavenly Father who loved us so much that He sacrificed His son Jesus to die in our place. With this example of sacrifice, how can we not respond and also make the sacrifices necessary that are called for in being a Dad? Our heavenly Father yearns to spend time with us, share life with us and shape us to be more like Him so that we may bare much fruit for the sake of others. Without the Hope of Christ all would be loss. But one of the great rewards of a relationship with Christ is peace and joy amidst sacrifice and the uncertain storms of life. By spending time in prayer, going to God for wisdom, and relinquishing all to Him, being a father can be an amazing journey. The greatest counsel I could give to any Father is to rely on your Heavenly Father, who knows all, sees all, and will direct our path if we allow him to do so. As it states in Proverbs: 3:5 *"Trust in the Lord with all you heart, and do not lean on your own understanding. In all your ways acknowledge Him, and He will direct your Path."* May this be so for all of us.

To the Fathers and to all who are reading this, God Bless you.

About David Lacine

After 34 years in the insurance industry, Dave sensed the call to develop C12 Groups in the Chicago area. C12 Group works with Christian Business Owners to steward their businesses to the Glory of God. Dave's business experience has been in agency expansion and growth, mergers and acquisitions, as well as small business growth and planning. He has held positions as president of two different firms and is also a past president of the largest insurance state association for independent agents in Illinois.

Along with his business background, Dave has been involved in leadership with small groups, couples groups, marriage ministry, and has led retreats for leaders with a focus on spiritual disciplines and development. Dave has also mentored high school students, and has served as president of the board for Emmaus Ministries in Chicago, which ministers to broken lives of men in the inner city. Dave's passions have also included short term missions which has taken him to China and working with church leaders in the Dominican Republic. He is a certified Spiritual Director.

Dave's desire is to see leaders in business develop to their true capacity not only in the business world, but personally and spiritually, to be all that God has called them to be.

Dave and Robin, his wife of forty years, reside in Downers Grove and have two grown children, along with four grandchildren. They are members and active in leadership at Christ Church of Oak Brook.

David Lacine | C12 Group Chair – Chicago | www.C12Chicago.com

https://youtu.be/GC-2f3TrKLg

53

Godly Men
Make Godly
Fathers

The Blessing of Christian Family and Father

By Brian P. Swift

I was blessed to be raised Catholic and taught a Christian lifestyle from my mother, father and grandparents. I also was fortunate to go to parochial grammar and high schools in a time where I was taught by nuns and the Christian Brothers of Ireland who reinforced the Christian values I was learning and living. My Christian faith and beliefs were really tested when I was 17 and broke my neck.

Now that I have three kids looking back to when I was 17 seems like being a good Christian was easy compared to the duty and understanding I have now.

I believe most fathers feel they understand what being a good Christian father means, just like I did. Unfortunately my beliefs were based my current understanding and beliefs of what being a Christian father meant.

As a Christian father I realized that being a good Christian or teaching your children how to be a good Christian couldn't be rushed. We must teach this wisdom and lead by example. With God's grace I ask for the guidance and strength to do the best I can with the bad and savor the good times because there is no stopping either. Your child will grow up and your roll will be redefined and revealed many times over. That is the double edged sword of fatherhood.

As a Christian father the greatest commandment in Scripture is this: "*Love the LORD your God with all your heart and with all your soul and with all your strength*" (Deuteronomy 6:5).

As a young man I understood what being a Christian was based on my previous school teachings, my mother's examples and motherly advice. Like most men the days go by fast and your routine goes from week to week and month to month without much thought going into my relationship with Christ.

I go to work every day and work hard. I go to church on Sundays, I am honest, I don't break the law, I help others and try to give back and I am a good husband. I must be a good Christian. Even after having several kids you view yourself in a similar fashion.

As your kids get older you start to realize that the rules, morals, and commandments you live your life by are the same ones you must impress on your children. I found ways to talk about them when I sat home and when I walk along the road, or other times I could fit it in.

At some point I realized it was my responsibility to provide my children with the wisdom and ways of being a good Christian. The training is designed to make clear to children the manner of life they are intended for. I realized that planning and starting a child's early Christian education is of great importance. A wise parent seeks to make obedience desirable and attainable by love and gentleness.

As a Christian father I am an instrument in God's hand. The whole process of instruction and discipline must be that which God commands and authority should be brought into constant and immediate contact with the mind, heart, and conscience of children. This must be an intentional act.

I realize that creating a relationship between my children and

God needed to be a larger part of my duties as a Christian father. It was not the school's responsibility, not the churches responsibility and it was not going to happen by osmosis.

As a father, I never presented myself as the ultimate authority or as one who has all the answers. I knew I had to learn more than I knew. I had to be a better example than I was being, not just to my kids but to all the people I came in contact with. I needed to be a better man of faith, a man of courage, a man of example.

It is a given that a father should not just love his children but lead them as well. If the parent is a true genuine Christian, then the parent should be overflowing with love, since love is from God. Love should be the first priority for the Christian parent.

A Christian parent has the responsibility for providing for one's family. No exceptions!!! No excuses!!! One of the greatest things a father can do for his child is to lead them to knowledge of Christ Jesus. If you do not place Christ first, then do not be surprised if your child does not.

I came from a very disciplined background. I knew the rules and the consequences, fair but firm. *"It is for discipline that you endure; God deals with you as with sons; for what son is there whom his father does not discipline?"* (Hebrews 12:7).

There is a biblical call for discipline. This requires the parent to set guidelines and to consistently uphold them. If there is anything that I learned from my time coaching and raising three kids, it was that children would test the limits of what you say and what you will do. Children left to their own whims will follow every flashy, shiny thing available to them. By the time they find that the flashy, shiny thing that tempts them is dangerous, it is many times too late.

As a Christian father it was my responsibility to be like a buffer. This simply means I was not to totally insulate them but try to keep away bad influences from my children. This may mean that I may need to cut out my child's ties to bad influences. These bad influences can be bad, music, television shows, certain Internet sites, friends who are troublemakers, or activities, which may lead the child away from godly principles

As your children get older you realize as a Christian father you must not only talk the talk but you must walk the walk. One of the best ways of providing Godly instruction for your child is for you to be a living example of what the Christian life should be

I knew I needed to grow in my faith, my knowledge and in my understanding of Christianity. I sought out fathers who were like-minded. This led me to commit to attending a small group. We got together in the church basement, watched the Christian movie Courageous and then talked about it. This lasted several months and when we were finished I realized there was so much more I was responsible for and so much more I could be doing.

I shared so many ideas and thoughts with my wife and she felt the same way. We decided to have a small group at our home. We had several couples that were looking to grow in our faith, knowledge and relationship with God. I know the more I grew the better I would be at leading my family. I was learning so many things about myself but also about the path I must pave for my family's life. Acknowledging Gods blessings became a daily function in my family.

I realized that I had to continue to learn about Christianity and what the Lord Jesus wants in order to grow in my faith and understanding. Not only did I want to learn more but also I realized that part of my purpose was to be a steward of the knowledge I was learning.

I also learned that it was not easy being a steward to my kids and family. My responsibility goes far beyond that. I had to take ownership and had the responsibility of being held accountable.

This level of thinking was a game changer for me. The best way for me to describe it is; it's like being a good high school athlete and waking up for practice and stepping on to the field of a Division One team. It's like being an excellent in-house or park district ball player and entering a true travel team tournament. Yes, I like you might too, thought I was doing all the right things. I thought I was working hard, preparing, I was committed and on top of my game.

Guess what, the game changed and just got bigger. There is way more at stake, the field is huge, the players are bigger, faster and stronger. Your confidence might even be waning. More importantly you're not playing for the name on the back of your jersey anymore. You're playing for the name on front of the jersey and its Gods team.

It is not a five or seven game series. It is one important game, the game of life and eternity.

Remember in the beginning of Genesis, God creates everything and puts Adam in the Garden to work it and to take care of it. It is clear that man was created to work and that work is the stewardship of all the creation that God has given him.

This is the fundamental principle of biblical stewardship. God owns everything; we are simply managers or administrators acting on his behalf. Therefore, stewardship expresses our obedience regarding the administration of everything God has placed under our control, which is all encompassing.

Stewardship is the commitment of one's self and possessions to God's service, recognizing that we do not have the right of control over our property or ourselves. Nothing really belongs to us. God owns everything; we're responsible for how we treat it and what we do with it.

We are called as God's stewards to manage that which belongs to God. While God has graciously entrusted us with the care, development, and enjoyment of everything he owns as his stewards, we are responsible to manage his holdings well and according to his desires and purposes.

We are all stewards of the resources, abilities and opportunities that God has entrusted to our care, and one day each one of us will be called to give an account for how we have managed what the God has given us.

We are called to exercise our dominion under the watchful eye of the Creator managing his creation in accord with the principles he has established.

As Christian fathers in the 21st century, we need to embrace this larger biblical view of stewardship, which goes beyond our possessions, church budgets or building projects, though important; it connects everything we do with what God is doing in the world.

We need to be faithful stewards of all God has given us within the opportunities presented through his providence to glorify him, and to serve the common good and further his Kingdom.

Then God said, "Let us make man in our image, after our likeness; and let them have dominion over the fish of the sea, and over the birds of the air, and over the cattle, and over all the earth, and over every creeping thing that creeps upon the earth." So God created man in his own image.

Collectively, we are stewards of the earth; each of us has opportunities and resources at our disposal that others do not have. You may own property to which no one else holds title. However, understanding that stewardship is collective requires us to find ways in which we can collaborate with others to make the resources in our possession work for the good of all as intended by God. All the resources at our disposal should help us to fill the earth and subdue it for the Glory of God.

The same can be said for helping a neighbor repair his house or care for his lawn, or lending tools to someone in need. Our time, talents, and possessions are all resources that should be shared.

The primary purpose of all creation is twofold: to give glory to God and to serve man's needs in preparation for the beatific vision of heaven. Because stewardship is collective, the service provided to man by a particular resource is not intended for only one man. Rather, the resources of the earth are intended for all humanity, and our use of them should reflect this solidarity.

In other words, it's not just what we use it for, it's also how we use it. For example, a car is intended to get us from one point to another. If we run stoplights and race at excessive speeds, we endanger the lives of others. In the same way, when we use resources for our own good, we must always keep in mind the common good.

Man's dominion over inanimate and other living beings granted by the Creator is not absolute; it is limited by concern for the quality of life of his neighbor, including generations to come; it requires a religious respect for the integrity of creation.

Christian stewardship is the only way we fulfill these commands of God. Our Lord challenges us to consider the dignity and freedom of each person. We must not think of other people as "problems" or as "expendable resources." Rather, we must recognize the fundamental rights of every human person; the right to life, adequate housing, clothing, food, and moral respect

Here are some questions you should think about. Do you have family prayer? Do you have family devotions? Do you read spiritual books to your children? Life is tough. Don't sugar coat things for your children. Tell them about the complexities and problems of life at an age-appropriate level and show how God has helped you through the tough times of life. Provide a moral foundation.

Outside of God, there exists no perfect father. But, that should not stop us from trying to be the best fathers that we can be. Can you imagine homes where fathers did what they were supposed to do as fathers? This would lead to certain changes in our culture. We would have children who would feel confident about themselves living in a supportive family environment.

Will you take the challenge to be the Christian father that God has called you to be and call out the man and woman in your child?

About Brian P. Swift

Brian is a Chicagoan. He broke his neck thirty-six years ago while playing football with his friends on a sunny, chilly day after Christmas, 1979, at the age of seventeen. As he found the courage and strength to recover, graduate from high school, earn his college degree, and earn his Juris Doctor degree as a quadriplegic, through his faith and family. He also found his purpose: to achieve more than expected and to aspire to the best he can be.

After spending seventeen years in corporate sales and management he wrote his first book; *Up Getting Up is the Key to Life*. He shares his personal paradigm for mental, emotional, and spiritual recovery and facing the challenges of life as quadriplegic. It is the author's hope to inspire those with similar injuries and give hope to their medical caregivers, family, and loved ones. His second book is *The Unofficial Guide to Fatherhood* and his third book is *Go Ask Your Dad*.

The father of three adopted children and a husband of over 27 years, Brian developed his strategy of success, CIA: Commitment, Integrity, and Attitude. With his engaging style and practical wisdom, Brian will leave you invigorated to face your own struggles with hope, faith, and purpose! He is also a certified John Maxwell Coach and speaker.

After co-Authoring his third book he started a non-profit called Swift Outdoor Accessible Recreation: SOAR. SOAR offers programs, services and equipment to improve the emotional and physical quality of life for people with disabilities, families, and individuals in need by creating outdoor accessible environments. www.soarnonprofit.com

Brian's books, *UP Getting UP is the Key to Life, The Unofficial Guide To Fatherhood* and *Go Ask Your Dad* are available at his web site.

www.brianpswift.com

Children are Mirrors

By Brian E. Panichelle

The Lord has blessed my wife Heather and me with six healthy children. We are thankful for the mercy he has shown us in raising our children. As one may imagine six children bring about lots of work, entertainment and situations that may not be as frequent in other families.

My wife and I homeschool our children at least until they reach high school age. Then, they can decide if they want to go to public school, technical training or some type of dual enrollment with a community college.

Beginning about the age of twelve they begin venturing into the public school system for band and choir; music is well loved in our home. The children also are involved in community sports and other programs, so there is always much to do. At the time of this writing, my oldest is about to turn twenty-one and my youngest ten.

We strive to be involved in all of our children's activities. We are soccer, scout, baseball, dance, band and choir parents to name a few. This too has been a blessing to our family as we made many contacts in the community that we most likely would not have otherwise made. My wife and I made many friends because of our children, an experience I would expect is not uncommon. Having such a large family and homeschooling we tend to draw a bit of attention. Whether it is because of our large van or just the number of people and volume of kid we arrive with at an event, we are used to being a bit odd compared to those around us. But, nonetheless, the LORD has blessed us with many friends and acquaintances to whom we hopefully are a witness and we minister to them all.

Over the years, I have been asked on more than one occasion what advice I might have for a new father. In this chapter, I will share with you what I share with others who ask me this question. I hope you find the response helpful and encouraging for that is how it is intended.

Remember when you found out that you were going to be a dad? It was exciting, right? Exciting in many ways, both positive and negative. The thought of being a dad inspires thoughts of greatness and fears about weaknesses. Children are a blessing from the LORD. This too in positive and negative ways. The Psalms are full of verses regarding children such as Ps 127:3-5. In the new American Standard Bible it reads, *"Behold, children are a gift of the LORD, the fruit of the womb is a reward. Like arrows in the hand of a warrior, so are the children of one's youth. How blessed is the man whose quiver is full of them."* This passage shows us that indeed children are a gift of the LORD, but it also implies that we as fathers have a responsibility to train and direct them in their ways.

I would expect that the reader has been told that they are just like their father or mother. We often times are a reflection of our parents, grandparents, older siblings and others who have had an influence in our lives.

Here in lies the interesting part and what I tell those who ask me for words of wisdom when becoming a father. I tell them to be ready, children are a giant mirror! The problem can be is that sometimes we don't like what we see in the mirror.

As a father, your children will expose and lay bare all the things you don't like about yourself! If the father is honest and attentive, he will recognize that the traits of his child, the tone of voice, irreverence, haughtiness, etc. all come from him. We may get frustrated with the words they use, their tones of voice that they employ, the things they do and don't do...

But, if we are honest we will see ourselves in their short comings. Be ready, you will find out from your children exactly what you don't like about yourself, what your faults and sins are. Children are like God's Law, they show us our sin and remind us of our need for a savior. The Savior, the only begotten son of God, the Lord Jesus Christ, who has humbled himself and lived perfectly for us and who took the Father's wrath for our sin, died and was raised again.

This is The Savior who now sits on high at the right hand of the Father and rules all things for the glory of God and the good of his people.

As much as we are charged as fathers with teaching our children as in Deuteronomy 6:1-9. Our children teach also are teachers for us. Children are a blessing from God because they direct us to The Savior of His people. They drive us to our knees and to live by faith. God uses our children to sanctify us as much as we are to instruct them in faith and sanctification.

This all probably sounds more discouraging than encouraging, but one's hope must be in the LORD. As Psalm 103 says, *he puts our sins far away from us, as far as east is from west. He shows us mercy. This is how we are to instruct our children, in mercy and in grace by making our lives a living sacrifice to the LORD.* (Rom. 12) As we live our lives before the face of God, when we look to the LORD, we see the mercy and grace and perfection of Jesus. We also see more and more of our sin as the LORD makes us alive in Christ, and gives us eyes to see and ears to hear.

As a father, you will struggle with your shortcomings and sins that your children reflect back at you. Our job is to be conformed to the likeness of Christ, to put our desires to death, that we may live in Christ, to keep our eyes fixed on him and the mercy he has shown, this is what we need to reflect to our children, and the LORD will bless and reflect these same things back at us from them.

So the reader at this point is wondering, "How can one do this?" There are practical and simple instructions throughout the Word of God. Romans 12:2 says *we must be transformed by the renewing of our minds.* Psalms 1, 119 and others tells us to make the Word of God our study all the day. Proverbs tells us that fear of the LORD is beginning of Wisdom. Solomon tells us in Ecclesiastes to fear God and keep His commandments, because this applies to every person.

As fathers we must flee! Flee not as the world flees from our responsibilities and from our families, but flee to the cross of the savior. Flee to the word of God which restores the soul. Flee to our merciful father who protects us and keeps us, who instructs us and cares for us. We are to flee to the means of grace, prayer, bible reading, and Christian fellowship. We are going to fall short, as does everyone.

We must rely on his grace, not passively or in a no worries, don't think about it kind of way, but in a follow Jesus kind of way. If we understand how broken we are, and understand that we cannot repair our relationship with God and we understand that we don't have to because that is why Jesus Christ became a man, lived perfectly and died for our sins. That we will have eternal life with HIM. Then we can sing with the Psalmist that our cup truly overflows. We can have confidence that as we seek HIM, our children will follow. The God of grace and mercy WHO has saved you, also promises to work grace and faith in the hearts of your children.

Having four children who are teenagers or older at this point is quite a challenge. They reflect more and more of my sins to me. I don't know about you, but my sins frustrate and anger me. Think of when Nathan the prophet went to King David to confront him about Bathsheba. (2 Sam. 12) Nathan tells David of a rich shepherd who coveted the lone and best sheep of a poor shepherd and how the rich man stole it and gave it to a traveler. David was full of fury, then Nathan told him that David is the rich man.

Often we see our sins in our children, we get anxious, excited and fearful for them. We get angry at our own failings and, we get angry at God. How could God let this happen to me? Well brother, I will tell you. We are all sinners, God uses this to bring us low, to repentance. To bring us to the cross where Christ takes our burden! God brings these challenges about for our good and the good of our children. His mercy is everlasting, his promises are sure. It is unjust for us to take our anger for our sins out on our children. We must remember we are looking in a mirror. If we don't like what we are seeing, we need to change it. We ourselves cannot change it, but our Heavenly Father can and does!

Thankfully, to others our children often reflect our Heavenly Father's work in their lives. The LORD has been gracious. Though he continues to work to conform me to his likeness, he also is working in my children. My older children are members of the Church, they have credible professions of faith and have an impact for Christ in their circles of influence. God has been faithful in bringing my children to faith in him. I have failed as a father many times and in many ways. Each time, I strive to throw myself at the mercy of God.

We as fathers will fail a lot, our Heavenly Father, does not fail, he will not leave us nor forsake us. His mercy is everlasting. He will complete the good work which he has begun in us and in our children. He will build the house and it will not be in vain. We must be transformed--made alive, brought back from the depths of sin and renew our minds. We must study his law, HIS WORD which restores the soul again (Psalm 19), and our Lord God will conform us to His image.

About Brian E. Panichelle

 Brian E. Panichelle was born and raised in Southwestern Pennsylvania. He is the older of two children. He is the husband of one wife. He and his wife Heather met at Geneva College, where they both obtained Bachelor Degrees in Business administration. Brian is a Ruling Elder in the Reformed Presbyterian Church of North America.

The LORD has blessed Heather and Brian with six healthy children. Brian has been self-employed most of his adult life. He aids Heather in homeschooling their children. Brian has taught several business and computer classes at the County Community College and has successfully completed and trained the Referral Institutes Certified Networker Program. Brian also enjoys speaking to young people. He has led seminars for 4-H and has spoken at multiple youth events. Brian is a member of several Chambers of Commerce and has helped deliver Chamber education programs in his local Jr. and Sr. High Schools.

As a Ruling Elder Brian serves by teaching and governing his local church and also serves in various capacities in Presbytery and Synod. He and his family enjoy volunteering their time together for the Food Bank and the Salvation Army as well as helping neighbors, friends, family and going on mission trips.

Brian's burning desire is to hear when the time comes, "Well done good and faithful servant, enter into your Master's rest."

Contact:

https://www.facebook.com/brian.panichelle

https://www.linkedin.com/in/brianpanichelle/

Parenting help from _THE Helper_!

By Paul Gray

This chapter is only for people who ever have had troubles in their parenting (and other aspects of life). It's only for those who need help from time to time. It's for single parents (and married parents) who have one (or more) kids, and who get worn out. It's for parents who sometimes get weary. It's for parents (and grandparents) who are burdened by their kid's (and their own!) choices, temptations and the things the world throws at them.

Oh! You're still reading. Yeah, it's for me too!

I have three wonderful children and an equally wonderful wife. Included in that group are a wonderful son-in-law and daughter-in-law and 6 superlative grandchildren. If you're wondering why I used the strongest description for my grandkids...you probably don't have grandkids☺

All ten of them (and I) have had challenges...and good times. Sometimes the good times come out of the challenges! I was 28, 31, and 36 when our kids were born. We were surprised to find that babies don't come with an instruction manual! Grandkids are easier for a lot of reasons--we now have experience...and they can usually go home with their parents after a while!

My wife and I each tried our best in parenting, drawing on our (very different) childhoods and remembering how our parents parented us.

But we never really knew what the goal of parenting is. Have you ever thought about that?

I've decided that for me, the goal is *loving unconditionally*. I could really end this article now!

Loving your kids, your spouse, and everyone unconditionally is what life is all about for me. I'm embarrassed to admit that concept wasn't on my radar 40 years ago. Unfortunately, I mainly just wanted to get my needs met.

My wife has always loved unconditionally. She expresses unconditional love all the time. I now know that is not "natural" – it's supernatural and it's Jesus in us living His life through us and as us. Jesus loved unconditionally. Even when people were doing the worst to Him, He prayed "Father, forgive them. They don't know what they're doing."

That wasn't always my first thought in parenting. Things happen. Kids don't do what we want. They put themselves in positions to be harmed…and harm others. They embarrass us.

Life can be hard. We can get worn out, weary, burdened… We even come to the end of our rope. That's because we have an enemy…and we have a Helper. If we don't know about those two entities, we literally live in the dark and don't know that we're living in the dark. We fight a battle we don't know we're fighting against an invisible foe. We don't know what we don't know.

Let's see where this started. How about at the beginning?

When God (Father, Son and Holy Spirit) created human beings as their ultimate creation in their image and likeness, the first couple lived in total union and oneness with Jesus, The Father, and The Holy Spirit. The five of them enjoyed amazing fellowship and community in the divine triune circle dance of God's nature--agape love--and everything that flows from that love: joy, peace, patience, kindness, goodness, gentleness, faith, compassion, mercy, grace, and so much more...always under the control of the Spirit's power.

That's the very community that Jesus included us all in by His finished work at the cross! That Community is what Jesus made possible for each of us right now today by his finished work at the cross. Various Christian communities use different names to describe it: Union; Oneness; Fellowship; Perichoresis; Walking (living) in The Spirit; Abiding in Christ; etc.

Living in that community is our greatest need as a Parent, Mom or Dad, Grandparent, friend...or even acquaintance.

It's very hard, though, because we have this enemy who wants to control us and keep us from that Special Community. That enemy is the *voice* Adam and Eve heard in the garden. It's the voice we hear that tempts us to get our needs met apart from God. Various Christian communities use different names to describe it: The Evil One; Satan; The Deceiver; The Accuser; The Enemy; Beelzebub; Old Scratch; The Tempter; The Devil; Diablos; Ophis; The Prince of the Air, The Ruler of the World, etc.

All parents (and grandparents) need to know that even though we want to be the very best parents possible, we have a crafty (but defeated) enemy who comes to steal, kill, and destroy the abundant life that we want to have with and for our offspring. He continually lies to us in the attempt to deceive us into believing that his way is best.

Fortunately, we're not left helpless! Our Helper is infinitely stronger than he who is in the world!

That voice is loud and can be very convincing and scary. I picture an ordinary person like you or me who gets the opportunity to tour a prison. We walk down the hall on death row. There are people behind bars who can't get to us and have no power over us.

73

They know they will soon be gone. But…they can yell at us, lie to us, insult us, tempt us, accuse us, and attempt to deceive us. Their voices are very real. At that moment they are our enemy. They would like to harm us.

But we have a choice. We can listen to the bad voices…or we can listen to The Teacher who lives in us.

The Christian band "Mercy Me" has a song called "Greater is the One Living Inside of Me" and it has several great lines. One of the lines is, "I hear a voice and He calls me redeemed / When others say I'll never be enough / And greater is the One living inside of me / Than he who is living in the world."

That's The Voice we can listen to for REAL help!

Without God's help, parents are left to their own best intuition, self-help books, parenting classes that may or may not be teaching God's ways, and other people's ideas and suggestions. They may have some good ideas, but they also may be misguided and misdirected…IF they aren't teaching Infinite Wisdom.

Fortunately, Infinite Wisdom is available! It's closer than the very air we breathe! The Holy Spirit of Christ…whom Jesus calls "The Helper" and "The Teacher," and whom Christians call "The Third Person of the Trinity," lives in us, wants to teach us, and will always point us to Christ. The Holy Spirit continually reveals to us the Righteousness of Christ which He imputed to us in His finished work at the cross.

We have that Wisdom available now, real time, 24-7! He invites us to come to Him to learn wisdom for our parenting and every-day living. We can access it, employ it, and use it not only in our parenting but in every area of our life. The writer of Hebrews urges us to "come near to the throne of grace." We don't have to go far to reach the Throne of Grace! It's closer than the air we breathe!

1 Corinthians 6:19-20 *Do you not know that your body is the temple of the Holy Spirit who is in you, whom you have from God,*

and you are not your own? For you were bought at a price; therefore glorify God in your body and in your spirit, which are God's.

Jesus knew in advance that we would have troubles in our parenting (and all aspects of our life). He knew we'd need help. He knew that like every single parent with one or more kids, we'd get worn out. He knew that all parents will get weary. He knew that all parents would be burdened by their kid's (and their own!) choices, temptations and things the world throws at them.

Jesus knew in advance the biggest challenge my wife and I would have in our parenting. That came in 2008 when our son-in-law, Travis, experienced the recurrence of cancer.

Travis grew up in the church where I was the founding senior pastor. When Travis was an aspiring professional baseball player playing the summer before his senior year in high school, he contracted Ewing's Sarcoma. That cancer typically occurs in children and young adults. It often begins in the legs. It started in Travis's right thigh. He spent a good portion of his senior year in high school at a hospital where he had more than half of his quad muscles removed. His baseball career was over.

Subsequently he recovered and the cancer went into remission. He went to college and seminary, married my daughter and became our youth pastor and potential senior pastor. He and I were close friends and had much in common. He and Molly had eight years of marriage together.

Because of the chemo and radiation during his first bout with cancer, he was unable to have children. He and Molly adopted a wonderful little boy in 2006.

In June of 2008 the cancer came back with a vengeance. Travis's right leg was amputated immediately and from then through December he had chemo and radiation at the hospital for 5 days every third week.

Needless to say that was a huge change in their family life. Each time he was in the hospital, our daughter stayed with him and we kept our grandson.

By the end of December the cancer was again in remission. Except it wasn't. A week after the remission report, he could feel the cancer pain again. This time it rapidly spread throughout his body.

Travis (and our daughter) spent all but a few days between December 31 and May 5th at the hospital. They "moved" into our house where our grandson had his own room and Travis and Molly had a room which they used the few days he was able to come home. Each of those times ended up with emergency ambulance rides back to the hospital…an hour away.

Travis graduated to the 'Life After' on May 6, 2009. It's been our pleasure and privilege for Molly and our grandson to live with us ever since.

From July 2008 until May 2009, my wife and I made the two-hour round trip with our grandson to the hospital to be with Travis and Molly* each evening. The kids in Travis's youth group at our church came en masse many evenings, bringing lawn chairs, coolers with snacks and drinks, and had "youth group parties" in Travis's hospital room.

During that time the church also had numerous prayer meetings which were devoted to praying for Travis's recovery. Many of us, including myself, believed he would recover.

But he didn't.

During that whole process, I was the pastor at the church where Travis grew up, and our families attended. During my own grief, I ministered to the rest of the church…and they ministered to me and our family.

During that whole process…and afterwards, I had the privilege of being husband, father, grandfather and father-in-law to our

76

extended families. I was trying to help and comfort them all…while I needed help and comfort myself.

That was by far the hardest period of any of our lives.

The one thing that we all did during that time was to get our strength from and depend upon Jesus.

We were tired, exhausted, perplexed, struggling with our faith, weary and heavy laden, and in need of rest. We needed mercy and grace and help in our time of need.

From what I learned during that time, I want to give you "Seven steps on how to make it through a horrific parenting situation."

Step One: *Come to Jesus*

Steps two through seven: Repeat Step One!

For us, there was really only one step that provided any real help-→ *Come to Jesus.*

Hebrews 4:16 says, *"Let us therefore come boldly to the throne of grace, that we may obtain mercy and find grace to help in time of need."*

What does *"Come to Jesus"* mean? It certainly may mean different things for different people. I get that.

For us, it started with knowing Jesus.

In the New Testament, in The Gospel of Matthew chapter 1 and verses 27-32 Jesus resumed talking to the people, but now tenderly. *"The Father has given me all these things to do and say. This is a unique Father-Son operation, coming out of Father and Son intimacies and knowledge. No one knows the Son the way the Father does, nor the Father the way the Son does. But I'm not keeping it to myself; I'm ready to go over it line by line with anyone willing to listen.*

"Are you tired? Worn out? Burned out on religion? *Come* to me. *Get away with me and you'll recover your life. I'll show you how to take a real rest. Walk with me and work with me—watch how I do it. Learn the unforced rhythms of grace. I won't lay anything heavy or ill-fitting on you. Keep company with me and you'll learn to live freely and lightly."*

So in Jesus's words, "*Coming* to Jesus" means *RESTING!*

As we simply hang out with Jesus (The Mystery that the Apostle revealed to us in Colossians 1:27 – *Christ in us, the hope of glory) we're able to rest from our work (striving to gain and maintain a right relationship with God and living life by our own efforts in our own power).*

We take a real rest and simply walk with Him and "work" with Him as He leads, guides and empowers us. We watch HOW HE DOES IT.

In the process we learn the unforced rhythms of grace and the result is that we start to live freely and lightly.

How, exactly did He do that? He told us that He didn't do or say anything except what The Father told Him to do and say.

I understand that's what He wants for us…in every area of our life; Parenting, Marriage, Work/Career, Education, Social, EVERYTHING!

As we become aware of Christ in us, then we're set free from having to figure out how to do things. We simply tune in to Him 24-7 (scripture calls that "praying without ceasing"), and continually ask: "*Jesus, what do you want me to do here? What do you want me to say?" What do you want me to know about what's going on with this other person?"*

Then we listen, and obey what we hear; IT'S THAT SIMPLE.

It's not easy, though! I forget to tune in to Him! I tend to want to do things my own way in my own strength! I sometimes listen to the enemy without realizing it. When I do those things, my parenting, husbanding, pastoring, and "friending" are never as good as they can be.

But you know what? Because of God's never ending unconditional love that never fails, and because of His mercy and grace...even when I settle for less than God's best and "mess up," He's always working things out for the best for me and everyone else!

That's how I want to parent...and do life with everyone else! I want to give them all "never ending unconditional love that never fails, mercy and grace."

That's the best example and advice for parenting...and life...that I've ever found.

Now occasionally, one of our kids would make a poor decision and we deemed some type of discipline was appropriate. When that happened, we always affirmed in advance that:

- We (and God) loved them unconditionally and any misstep they might make would never change that love
- Here's the "punishment" and here's why
- The purpose of punishment is always remedial...
  to restore

Then we did our best not to bring the situation up to them again as in "you always...or you never..."

Greek (the language the New Testament was written in) dictionaries seem to show that with any "punishment" that comes from God, the aim is "To get the good separated from the evil and to attract it into the communion of blessedness. Punishment may hurt, but it is like the fire which separates the alloy from the gold; it is like the surgery which removes the diseased thing; it is like the cautery which burns out that which cannot be removed any other way."

I mentioned earlier that kids can embarrass us. I've come to learn that if I get angry with my kids (or grandkids), and take that anger out on them because I feel they are reflecting poorly on me and embarrassing me-- then I'm the one who has a problem, not them.

God's "agape" unconditional love always does what's best for the other person. It doesn't focus on its own perceived reputation and image.

Now, did we always parent perfectly? No. Do we now relate to our grandchildren and our adult children perfectly? No.

That's why in all cases we're so thankful that

- *God's perfect love keeps no record of wrongs!* (1 Corinthians 13:5)
- *God's perfect love casts out all fear!* (1 John 4:18)
- *God is love!* (1 John 4:8, 16)

Galatians 5:6 The Message -- I suspect you would never intend this, but this is what happens. When you attempt to live by your own religious plans and projects, you are cut off from Christ, you fall out of grace. Meanwhile we expectantly wait for a satisfying relationship with the Spirit. For in Christ, neither our most conscientious religion nor disregard of religion amounts to anything. What matters is something far more interior: faith expressed in love.

In parenting (as in our marriages and every relationship) we can never go wrong by letting Christ in us express His unconditional love through us and as us. As we do, the watching world will know that we're His followers!

We can't go wrong with that!

~Paul Gray

In this chapter I have not peoples' real names per the family requests. Thank you for your understanding! ☺

About Paul Gray

Paul and his wife of 48 years, Kitsy, live in Lawrence Kansas where they continue to facilitate growing in grace at the church they founded in 1991, New Life in Christ. They have three wonderful grown children and 6 amazing grandchildren! *Convertible Conversations¸* a short week-day video series on a wide range of topics, are posted by Paul at *Online Community Church* on Facebook. *Notes from Papa* are also posted periodically at *God is For Me* on Facebook.

Before starting New Life in Christ, beginning in 1969, Paul was involved in a variety of businesses ranging from retail music stores to a long-distance telephone company, including Paul Gray's Jazz Place, a popular Lawrence, Kansas, jazz venue where he performed with his group, The Gaslite Gang. Concurrently, he served in the United States Army National Guard and Reserves for 24 years as a bandmaster.

In 1999 his church started a medical clinic for homeless individuals, The Heartland Medical Clinic, which continues to serve the medical needs of thousands of patients each year.

Paul Gray holds an education degree from the University of Kansas and a degree in theology from Global Grace Seminary.

His first book, *The Fishnet Experience* and musical recordings can be found at www.fishnetexperience.com.

Spiritual articles and videos can be found at www.godisforme.org.

You may contact Paul Gray at convertibleconversations@gmail.com.

On Being a Godly/Faithful Mentor

By William Fawcett Jr.

It was a very hot day in August as I sat on my patio overlooking the summery fields. I was waiting for my protégé to arrive. We are going to tar the driveway. We were supposed to start in the early morning. However, he chose not to arrive on time.

So, after waiting for about an hour I proceeded to resurface the driveway I used a syrupy tar coating that you may be familiar with. I had a large squeegee and it wasn't too difficult to sweep it back and forth and back and forth and back and forth.

However, my mind kept wandering to my tardy protégé. He should have been on time. I was paying him a good wage to do this job. And, he was missing an opportunity to learn something valuable for his life.

After finishing the job I reflected and looked upon the newly coated surface of our driveway. It looked great! I could smell the scent of the greasy tar and, I have always liked that smell.

Also, I was proud of the fact that the coating was applied as it should be. Because if one does not smear the coating properly, getting it into all the cracks and little places it will not be a good job. To do this, you must get the tar syrup into those cracks if not, it will create a nightmare in the following spring after winter. You know, with the freezes and the thaws?

Well, what happened to my protégé? He finally arrived about 3 p.m. in the afternoon. Wisely, he did not drive up to the house!

Of course, he could see the obvious, I had already done all of the work that he had promised to do with me earlier that day!

Now, this is the promise of God, "Forgive and it shall be forgiven you, forgive us our trespasses as we forgive those who trespass against us!"

As I was seated in a nice lawn chair admiring the work that had been completed I saw him walking up to the house.

When he arrived he said, Oh Bill, I am so sorry I couldn't get here!" He then used the common excuse of having had some sort of an emergency!

So, I asked him what, what was the emergency? He didn't really have a good answer he stammered and stuttered it was really quite embarrassing.

But, the most amazing question was this! In spite of asking my forgiveness for being late to the job, he actually asked me for an advance!

This young slothful late worker, he actually wanted paid for work that he had not done!

Here is where it gets pretty dicey, I remember feeling flushed with astonishment! And, then I said to him "Listen, you had the opportunity to be here to work with me to do this job! Did you not? He replied, "Yes, yes I did. But, Bill I had a problem!"

This is when I said to him your problem does not mean an emergency on my part nor does it mean that I should advance you anything for something that you have not done to earn!

Then, I said to him please young man listen to the words of Our Lord God as it is recorded in the Holy Bible, those who do not work should not eat!

You, young man did not work today.

Therefore, you should not receive anything!

Feeling a bit judgmental I asked him, "Why do you need the money?" He replied, I need it for a speeding ticket.

So I replied to him, "Did you get it while you were racing to my home to help me with this job?" No, he had NOT been ticketed that day but earlier in the month.

To this I told him, again, no. I'm not going to advance you anything. In fact, I will not be needing your services in the future.

My young Protégé was astonished at my frank words. He seemed to be lost in thought thinking that he thought that he could get away with this! Why? Why? Why?

Why do Millennials or anybody for that matter, think that they are owed something whenever they have a little problem or even a big problem in their lives?

Scripture clearly proclaims that we are to work! We are to do service for others but, particularly service for our Lord and God and Savior Jesus Christ.

Let me conclude with this. Let's be more committed to represent a disciplined example to the youth!

For many years, I have had the privilege, the awesome and God blessed honor of leading our family business. My sons also work with me in this business as well as my other family and non-family members. Together, we try to glorify our Lord and Savior Jesus Christ through our work and through our business!

Here, I want to reference the words of Holy Scripture! *And whatsoever you do it heartily as to the Lord and not unto man!* Colossians 3:23

About William Fawcett Jr.

William is Bell-View Brand Food Products President; it is located in ·Penn, Pennsylvania. He also serves as Director of Manor Bank, Irwin, Pennsylvania.

Bill and his wife, Linda have four (4) children and eight (8) grandchildren.

When Bill is not at the plant, he is at home on the family farm, *Fawcett Farview Farm*. He and his family work it together where they have beef cattle and grow their own hay feed and corn.

William is on the Trustee Board of First Evangelical Free Church 4001 University Drive McKeesport, PA 15132.

Contact Bill on Facebook. Copy and paste the following URL for the Facebook account for William Fawcett Jr.

https://tinyurl.com/yc872wms

HOPE Healing Others Potential Energy

By Dr. Ed Kropf

Children bring out feelings from the heart overflow and become words written down with pen and paper. Letters, poetry, and deep thoughts are all a way to express raw emotion. And, so I write and share some of my deepest thoughts and emotions concerning fatherhood in this chapter. Many of these things I have written to and for my children over the years.

During one of the most difficult times in my life, with my marriage of questionable strength and no concrete direction, I met the Lord Jesus Christ at an altar call. After I met the Lord Jesus my life was changed! I was given a renewed purpose and identity despite our marriage ending. I came to know Jesus as the Great Comforter. He turns everything to good for those whom He loves and calls according to his purpose. I hold deeply onto His promise in Romans 8:28-29 with my whole heart. In this promise I seek the blessings of an adverse prosperity. From this passage I draw so much. I am strengthened and blessed by God's Word to me. It makes me glad to share this with you because His Word is for everybody.

After our divorce, I found myself writing constantly. This endured the course of about five years. I wrote poems. I wrote daily letters to my children activity and emotional timelines our time together and our shared history. Some poems felt inspired to pen.

All of these memories I kept in notebooks, aware of the joy they would be to read in the future. In one of my more inspired works I reflected deeply on my life. I had made a transition from a wild stallion into a horse at peace that could be used the Lord Jesus to help others. I found a security in Christ and a change taking place within me daily.

For me, the good the Lord had in store for me became a Ministry. I administer Hope, an acronym which means Healing Others Potential Energy. I do this as a third-generation chiropractor. I've learned to utilize Functional Energy Medicine and Integrative Medicine in order to bring people HOPE. Each encounter with a patient is a blessing of healing which comes with lessons of growth and development. Don't forget those lessons, seek them out.

In my practice, I see daily the energy stolen from people who have to live with physical trauma, hidden infectious diseases, toxicity, and deep-rooted emotional issues and drug addiction typically from well-meaning medical doctors. All of which negatively affect the very well-being of their persona as well as interfere with their ability to bond with family and friends. They aren't living up to their potential well-being, which would enable them to manifest their God-given talents. They know it, but have either given up, simply given into their issues. Many find themselves on a merry-go-round with treatments, going from doctor to doctor looking for answers. Most often, I find that these problems are intertwined with many underlying components. I know they must be treated holistically and in an integrated sense. This concept is puzzling to people who are not in my profession but I like to try to help people understand.

In my opinion, the Lord Jesus continues to call people every day to receive miraculous physical and emotional healing to have wellbeing. This may not happen on their terms but on His. We need to be in a generally adaptable state to discern between God's will and our will, what direction He'd have us go from the self-centered pursuits. The word Hope expresses this. It captures the practice of counseling and helping to be a part of God's healing process, which heals others potential energy. Let me share just a couple of examples. Two patients were referred to me by a local church. Both cases had people that were stuck for more than 20 years because of emotional trauma and loss of Hope. The type of counseling, whereby people talk through their issues wasn't effective, not because of poor counselors, but due to the inability to hear and change. After less than a month, both of these patients stated they were improving with the same counselors! HOPE! I did my special treatment and "reset" their respective nervous and emotional systems back to "factory standards" out of fear and into growth.

I feel that the Lord can speak through each one of us as fathers to our children. We need to be open to his leading and direction through his holy scriptures and to have a sensitive heart to listen and follow the leading of the Holy Spirit. We fathers need to lose our pride and be broken by HIM and set the example of the Lord Jesus before our children. As a father and a believer in our Lord Jesus Christ my goal is to do everything I can to bring Glory to God and Lead my sons in the way of Christ.

A few years ago, at Christmas, I wrote a poem to my oldest son. It was called, *A Stone Along Your Path*. I am proud my son has chosen a direction that he has sought out in prayer and fasting before God. He is called into ministry. I get this, lol, I wanted him to follow me. My way was perfect in my eyes. Jesus knows my sons heart and direction for his future. Ultimately I wanted my sons to know the Lord, follow His teaching and direction. I got what I wanted even though it was different then my thoughts. For both of my sons, I have taught them that I am just one stone along their paths. I want them to know they are free to choose any direction. I have instructed my sons in the multiplicity of the options in their choices. I have always challenged them to consider and ask God for wisdom. It is sort of like a C drive in a computer. There can be fragmentation but, they can overcome fragmentation and be focused on their chosen paths.

As a chiropractic physician, I recognize what chronic stress does to people physically, as well as in their body, mind, and spirit. I am not exempt from chronic stress however as a physician I try to deal with it in a practical manner and as a Christian. One of my prayers brought me solutions and I received support from my family and patients. My good friend and confident Pastor Doug Lauffer taught me, or should I say reminded me, that the Bible jokingly retorts "physician heal thyself" (Luke 4:23). Instantaneously, I played it off when he reminded me of this. Of course, I know I should not be my own diagnostician or doctor; but, when he brought this to my attention I felt that I was literally stuck. At that time, I was preparing to go on a three-day educational experience in Tempe, Arizona. It was a seminar on the famous Brimhall treatment. I also knew that at the seminar I would be able to get some treatment from other doctors. It would not only be a learning experience, but also a wonderful time of healing.

At this seminar in January 2016, the Lord Jesus reminded me that we suffer for three (3) good reasons:

1. To get closer to God

2. To experience the healing that HE intends for us

3. To GO and to help others

After that seminar, I continued to apply the Hope methodology in my practice and was reinvigorated to be better in my life with the Lord, with my practice, and with my boys! Next week (8/24/17) I will provide a talk for an insurance company on stress and related physical problems. This was certainly not the direction I thought I'd go about two and a half years before, but with God anything is possible. Today, a week before the talk, my son helped put together the video presentation for the speech. I got to hold my grand-baby while we worked through the material.

As a result of my talk, a nurse with chronic bowel dysfunction and scheduled for complete large bowel resection was treated at the talk. She shared some bowel rumbling an hour after a simple treatment and made an appointment for the next day. I treated her. She texted me the very next day and my son was present to read of her marked improvement! It's a start. HOPE. She has a long recovery, however we have HOPE.

Another poem I wrote for my sons was inspired by the simple snowflake. Each snowflake has a design that is unique and special. No two snowflakes are the same. I've raised my sons with this in mind so that they would see themselves as unique and special and to treat each person they meet the same way. The Lord Jesus sees us from the inside out. He knows the intent, and motivation Our Lives. He understands our deepest thoughts and feelings. Wow! Try and conceptualize for a moment how we group and categorize people and don't see them as unique and special before God. Our children are different from us, period. God knows what's best for them, not us. Pray with your children to seek His plan and purpose for them and be HUMBLE.

To me, it is little wonder why our young people today have such a problem with not only accepting their own uniqueness but that of others. I want to model unconditional love because I am unconditionally loved by the Lord God. My goal has been to raise my sons like God has raised me in the Christian life. I received the milk of God's word and still have a childlike understanding of the things of God. Now I get vegetables ;-)

Over the years as I have grown in the Grace and knowledge of our Lord, God, and Savior Jesus Christ. As I follow Him I've learned that His path is not always a smooth path, I find it is a stony path. But through Jesus Christ I am able to walk this path. It is a path of Love. It's a path of faith, a path with many Stepping Stones. It's the path that I find I am directed and redirected according to the leading of the Holy Spirit. I need to be sensitive and recognize the weakness in my heart and also the strength of Satan's influence. After all, all men justify their actions, but the Lord ponders the heart!!! Often when I consider my own heart, or my own motivation for why I'm doing what I'm doing, I find pride at the center. And I'm then forced to step back and go another direction.

I try to remain sensitive to this truth as I live out each day and remember that God sent His angels to cover my back. And He is leading every situation He permits in my life. I trust God to direct my ways. Proverbs 3:5–6 state to trust in the heart in the Lord with all your heart and to lean not unto your own understanding and in all your ways acknowledge Him and He will direct your path. So, don't be wise in your own eyes because that's the attitude of pride. With this way of thinking I find that God uses everything and everybody to help me find my way. He doesn't always use Believers to touch my life. In some of my closest encounters with God, it has been unbelievers whom He used. As I've said before, it is the nature of living and being sensitive to the leading of the Holy Spirit at all times.

My son Louis has grown in his faith and I see that he gets it! He discerns God's will through the Scriptures and prayer. He'll also ask others for advice especially the elders in the Christian faith. He is open to receive wisdom and understanding from other men and women of God. Though these are fallen and imperfect people, he has learned as I've tried to teach: God will lead you in your life if you trust him and follow the principles that He has set forth in His Holy Scriptures.

Isn't it wonderful how the Scripture often shows you grace through our Lord Jesus Christ? Grace is yours even though you're imperfect. HE who first showed you grace continues to show you grace. As I encounter people, who have all fallen short of God's perfection, I can easily look at them in peace, love, affection and HOPE. Why? Well, the first three chapters of Romans have personally made me aware of how God see me. I'm forced to be brutally honest about my own condition. And, so I have enough improvement to accomplish in my own life. I'm too busy to be real fussy with other people's problems, especially if they don't ask for my help.

You may have heard it said "I am just a sinner saved by grace." To me, this means that when I look honestly at myself through the lens of the Holy Scripture I can understand that the hidden secrets of my black heart filled with evil thoughts. Not to mention, words and deeds left undone. How can I not be loving and understanding toward others? How can I ever condemn or judge others? Admittedly, it is a temptation to do so. The reason you ought not to is plainly stated by Jesus Himself; "*JUDGE NOT lest you be judged, for with what judgment you judge others you shall be judged."*

I love my sons unconditionally. I may not always and in all ways like them, nor what they do, but I can honestly say that every day I believe in God's perfect will and that he is leading my sons and me. He's leading us in love and affection by HIS grace.

It is at this point I must say that I have experienced a wonderful way of living, i.e. more kind, less judgmental, more patient, less impatient, more peace, less conflict. This is the kind of life that I am experiencing. It is a life worth living! Now, I look at my children, my entire family, my co-workers, patients and friends through this lens of grace. This is how I try to encounter everyone I meet. This pathway also prevents me from experiencing negative energy and a loveless lifestyle. It is the way that our Lord God intended us to live. God says LOVE, He doesn't command us to like. I think it best to not socialize with someone that would bring injury to my heart, just a word to the wise about personal boundaries.

Often, people say and do things which I do not like, which definitely includes my children. But, I am still expected to love. Love is forgiving, but doesn't affirm sin. So, often-times I need to inject a healthy dose of correction-in-love to help guide us as a family in the way of peace. Clearly, loving your children unconditionally doesn't mean you permit them to live in the negative energy of anger, lust for money, and the things of this world to the exclusion of personal growth and development. All of this intertwines with their relationships with others, so it is very important.

The unconditional love of God allows me to help and be persistent for my children. Whatever their needs, I will do my best to provide. A lot of prayer went and still goes into raising my children. If you give it your all without God helping you, then you'll a lot of your effort wasted. To me, the concept of HOPE equals feeding on Christ, being influenced by Christ, and influencing others with the nourishment that I get from Christ. Without hope there is no change, without change there is no hope. When this kind of lifestyle is lived one receives peace, love and harmony with other people on a much deeper level. This is true whether the other person is a believer or not! Christ spoke to believers and unbelievers all with the same hope, energy message.

Fathers, parents, please don't get frustrated and give up hope. When we see no change often we get discouraged. One evening my son showed me he understood this small fact, which is no small fact at all. Relationships being strained and working to develop deep communication with other people is a necessity for one's life. It is a philosophy I first adopted many years ago and talk about with my children. And, learning to do it in spite of the strain we have with others is hard, but it's what we were made to do. To me, enlightenment, in this regard, as a result of instruction, coupled with the stones of faith walking along life's pathway, my sons can experience the wondrous kaleidoscope and beauty of everybody they meet. How does that reflect the hope that they transmit to others? How does this influence their view of themselves, as well as others? Think about it, please think about it. When one looks at others with unconditional love does one want to experience more peace and understanding? Does not one become a better listener to other people?

For me this perspective has formed over decades of time. It is a transformation. Like the Bible says *"from glory to glory,"* we go from immaturity to being more mature in the Christian faith as we go along God's path. I went from a free range stallion to a saddled useable and functioning work-vessel of Christ.

The Peace of Jesus Christ surpasses any worldly comprehension of peace. It is a deep and abiding peace that can be the dominating power in my life in spite have anything happening around me. Permit me to share the following prayer:

God, oh Lord Jesus Christ through your incomparable love and grace, through your mercy and love, I can understand that all things work together for good to them who love you. Your love, oh Lord God, has made me a wealthy man. You have allowed me to experience Your unconditional love. Thank you for shaping me into a usable vessel. Please continue to shape me. Through your Son I know I am loved, I have worth, and I am an instrument of your peace and love. Amen.

People need not justify their actions with this kind of prayer in their hearts. People need not justify themselves when they know that they can come to God just as they are. They can't play games with God. They need to stop trying to because God, who is rich in unconditional love, as shone through the gospel of our Lord Jesus Christ, forgives!

Long ago, I waited for a computer program to defragment my hard drive. I watched its progress on the computer screen. It made me realize something. After a bit of time I realized I'm like that fragmented computer. And, I wrote the following: "Jesus is the GREAT defragmenter." Jesus never required sifting through thoughts and emotions before providing instant, as well as, perfect responses to any given situation. If we could see ourselves clearly, we would see how we have learned wrong from entertainment, parents, teachers, and preachers. To respond like Christ to that truth, we have to sort through our wants, needs, and desires. Then, we have to compare them to Scripture. In all honesty, it's a lifelong pursuit and one only available after joining Him in eternity. Try it. Jesus said, "I am the vine, you are the branches. Abide in me and I in you, and you will bear much fruit. For, apart from me you can do nothing." Is that not a liberating thought; 'we can do all things through Christ?' And that we are not alone? And also, that HE is with us along the stony paths of our Lives? Be liberated in knowing this!

God bless you and if you would like to reach out to me feel free to do so. I would love to talk to you and share more. I am always here to pray for you and with you. I need your prayers as well.

About Doctor Edward L. Kropf

Edward L Kropf Jr. is a Pittsburgh Pa. based third generation Chiropractic Physician. His grandfather also maintained an Osteopathic degree and studied herbal medicine in Europe. His father, also a Chiropractor, was recognized as an expert in x-ray interpretation. Doc Jr. Post-graduate degrees and interest are: Integrated Medicine, Functional Medicine, Wellness, and Concussions as related to accidents and sports.

Dr. Kropf has taught technique and provides wellness and health talks including anti-aging to groups, communities, organizations and professionals.

To date Doc's proudest accomplishment and passion involved raising and being a stepping stone in his sons' lives, current ages 21 and 20. He loves his children very much indeed. Not experiencing a close time/activity relationship with his own father, Doc took up the cross, listened and learned by great wisdoms in books and by others examples and spent every moment available sharing with his children. Long woods walks or asphalt jungle excursions made available opportunities to invoke life lesson wisdom into his boys.

Doc enjoys a healthy relationship with Jesus as his personal mentor. You can use his contact information to reach out to him.

https://www.facebook.com/kropfchiropractic/

Kropf Chiropractic
Address: 820 Cedar Ave, Pittsburgh, PA 15212
Phone: (412) 321-5231

Our Speech and Our Lives
By The Unnamed Author

Death and life are in the power of the tongue. In Proverbs Chapter 18 we find these words, "*A man's belly shall be satisfied with the fruit of his mouth; and with the increase of his lips shall he be filled. [21] Death and life are in the power of the tongue: and they that love it shall eat the fruit thereof.* [22]

At this point my life I consider myself an older teacher having had the privilege of being at teacher at several schools.

As a teacher I have tried to instruct a young scholars in the importance of language. I have taught them that words really do matter. Words are reflection of one's actions, words often times set in motion one's actions.

These words often start somewhere deep in one's mind or heart. These words can PROPEL and MOTIVATE individuals to great works or great evil works.

Therefore the author of Proverbs chapter 18 uses this kind of language that is to say that death and life, these extremes, are contained in the little member of the tongue. For example, a leader of a country can declare war with that tongue and many deaths will follow this announcement from a little tongue.

WITH the same tongue, a country's leader can declare peace and many lives will be saved, much destruction and devastation will be averted!

The Apostle James wrote on the death and life power of the tongue. OH, such a little member the tongue is but it can cause great good and great destruction!

Consider this passage taken from The Living Bible, James chapter three (3).

1-2 *Dear brothers, don't be too eager to tell others their faults, for we all make many mistakes; and when we teachers of religion, who should know better, do wrong, our punishment will be greater than it would be for others.*

If anyone can control his tongue, it proves that he has perfect control over himself in every other way. 3 We can make a large horse turn around and go wherever we want by means of a small bit in his mouth. 4 And a tiny rudder makes a huge ship turn wherever the pilot wants it to go, even though the winds are strong.

5 So also the tongue is a small thing, but what enormous damage it can do. A great forest can be set on fire by one tiny spark. 6 And the tongue is a flame of fire. It is full of wickedness, and poisons every part of the body. And the tongue is set on fire by hell itself and can turn our whole lives into a blazing flame of destruction and disaster.

7 Men have trained, or can train, every kind of animal or bird that lives and every kind of reptile and fish, 8 but no human being can tame the tongue. It is always ready to pour out its deadly poison. 9 Sometimes it praises our heavenly Father, and sometimes it breaks out into curses against men who are made like God. 10 And so blessing and cursing come pouring out of the same mouth. Dear brothers, surely this is not right! 11 Does a spring of water bubble out first with fresh water and then with bitter water? 12 Can you pick olives from a fig tree, or figs from a grape vine? No, and you can't draw fresh water from a salty pool.

13 If you are wise, live a life of steady goodness so that only good deeds will pour forth. And if you don't brag about them, then you will be truly wise! 14 And by all means don't brag about being wise and good if you are bitter and jealous and selfish; that is the worst sort of lie. 15 For jealousy and selfishness are not God's kind of wisdom. Such things are earthly, unspiritual, inspired by the devil. 16 For wherever there is jealousy or selfish ambition, there will be disorder and every other kind of evil.

17 But the wisdom that comes from heaven is first of all pure and full of quiet gentleness. Then it is peace-loving and courteous. It allows discussion and is willing to yield to others; it is full of mercy and good deeds. It is wholehearted and straightforward and sincere. 18 And those who are peacemakers will plant seeds of peace and reap a harvest of goodness.

About The Unnamed Author

This chapter is for all fathers who feel that life has been such that they cannot talk publicly about their experiences.

However, we wanted to give them a voice here and to edify each person who, for whatever reason, can't speak openly about their experiences and want to be anonymous.

Good, Good Father

By Paul Dimtroff

June is a month when many couples exchange vows of Holy Matrimony; to cherish, love and to honor each other "until death do us part". This signifies the beginning of a commitment and responsibility between the couple in upholding and sharing those vows throughout their years.

Witnessing the marriage ceremony and the exchanging of vows, love is the eyes and hearts of each bride and groom. Hold hands, making life long commitments to each other, in the presence of family and friends but most important, in the presence of the Lord, asking for his blessings.

"On that day, we witness a commitment between to two people who vow to love, cherish, honor one another in sickness and in health till death do us part. For a future that will be spent together. As stated in, Isaiah 26:3-4, *Trust in the Lord forever, for He is everlasting strength.*"

"*Being of one mind, having compassion for one another, being tenderhearted and courteous.... knowing you were called to do this, that you may inherit a blessing.*" 1 John 3:8-9

When we fall in love and are in love with the one who shares that feeling, we are blessed. When we experience the joy of becoming parents, we share in the responsibilities to properly raise, provide for and to educate our children, through sacrifices, hard work and a commitment to our faith.... Through these joys, as parents, we must remember it is our responsibility to honor and respect each other and to teach our children they have that responsibility to their parents.

Fathers have a life-long responsibility for protecting and caring for our wives and children. As fathers, we can accept nothing less of ourselves than to do our very best; to remain committed to our families

There is a beautiful song titled, *Good Good Father*, written by Pat Barrett and Tony Brown and often sung by Christian singers like, Chris Tomlin. It exemplifies the true meaning, nature and spirit of The Good Father and not our earthly father. It speaks of our true Father in Heaven. How wonderful it would be if we, as fathers, could be more like Him in love, in actions and in grace.

"I've heard the tender whispers of love in the dead of night
And you tell me that you're pleased
And that I'm never alone
You're a good, good father"

How many children never hear these words, never experience tenderness and compassion from our own earthly fathers? How many children wonder why their father never compliments with a tender word; encouraged by "a job-well done"; never 'lifted' upon his shoulders by his words of grace; have him say, 'no matter your struggles, I will always be there for you, to help, comfort and advise?

Most young parents, we are now always taught proper parenting. Many times it is a 'trial and error' procedure, left to our own devices or 'skill-set'; sometimes following the examples set by our own parents and others. Their child-rearing skills may not be the best examples of parenting. In most cases, parenting skills should not be 'a hand-me-down course'.

No doubt, many books have been written about Parenting, yet how many are read, studied or followed. There are no requirements to becoming parents. As the mores of society continue to change, we see children brought into a world void of the traditional family unit. Many times, the household is without a father, or without the mother. The joys, responsibility and burdens of raising a child is placed on a grandparent, the school or society.

What happened to some 'men'? Have they decided it's better to be free, without the commitment to a wife, a child, a home; he no longer wants the responsibility of making a life for them. So, what we see are too many of these 'men' in gangs, on drugs, dead, or in jail. Of course, then they don't have to worry about commitments; the decisions are made for them.

So 'men' what about the child? The soul that was conceived by you and another, two willing parties. Now will that child be abandoned, neglected, abused, allowed to wander without guidance or direction, without a mentor, a father?

In some cases, these children have the strength, spirit, and determination to overcome their environment, their circumstances. To look toward mentors, teachers, coaches, men of good character, men who will be their 'Brother's Keeper' who will believe in them, give them support and a faith in themselves and in the Lord. They say it only takes a little faith to move a mountain.

Men like Rev. Billy Graham, Rev. Franklin Graham, Rev. Dr. John Guest, Steelers Coach Mike Tomlin; Pirates Coach Clint Hurdle, former player and radio personality Tunch Ilkin; Rev. Dr. Ed Glover of Urban Impact and faith based programs throughout the country, similar to Man-Up Pittsburgh encourage and teach men to become stronger leaders in their homes. They, as well, as challenge men and fathers to address the needs of their families and communities; they inspire men to be their best, particularly when it comes to fatherhood.

The book, *The Unofficial Guide to Fatherhood* written by the hand of several authors makes the effort and succeeds in making the case for the importance for fathers to have a positive impact on the lives of their children.

The forgotten, abandoned, abused and unwanted child may never know the joy of accomplishment or their lost potential. An aborted life will never have that opportunity. It is a shame when a parent takes no interest or the time in their child's life; shows no love or affection, encouragement. Yet, there are those who know and love them and the way God 'holds' them.

If You Know Whose You Are, beautiful words written by Carol Lienhart tells us that, with our FATHER'S love there is success; no fear, that you are in His heart, that His arms are always open.

'If You Know Whose You Are.

If You Know God Made You Whole - Then Make No Plans For Failure.

If You Know Your Father's Heart - That He Loved You From The Start

If Your Faith Is In His Word – Not The Other Things You've Heard

If Your Plans Are To Succeed – You Have Everything You Need

If You Know Whose You Are'

As parents and fathers, it's our responsibility to guide our children, relieve their doubts of our love for them beginning at an early age. With the guidance of fathers, The Father and other mentors, we should answer their questions, provide suggestions and set the example for young men and women to follow.

Beginning with our own bodies and minds, we must decide what to expect of ourselves and what is expected of us. Do we allow others to set a poor example of us or our children? Do we become a beacon of light for their future; strive for excellence, exceptionalism, and hold ourselves above societal norms.

Each day we read of the ravages of drugs; young men and women dying from various additive drugs, murdered for a few dollars or not belonging to the right gang; all on the pretense of a misguided idea that getting 'high' will solve problems. Money is a driving force for many including those in state governments who have the conception that controlling various drugs will add to the coffers and allow for uncontrollable budgetary spending, at the expense of our youth and others.

We are all blessed when an individual succeeds in life, or fulfills a dream in spite of a parent's criticism. Many have felt that lack of encouragement; you're not smart enough; not good looking enough, not popular enough to make something of yourself... How sad it is when we encounter those reactions or comments.

Yet, many deal with this lack of support or encouragement. Each day we read or hear about a teenager who has decided to run away from home; or decided to commit suicide. Even adults find that rejection from those they love can be overwhelming and difficult to understand.

The recent news story of a distraught woman attempting suicide by jumping from a Pittsburgh bridge, yet was saved by a man who, on his way to umpire an upcoming baseball game, gave her his hand and reached out to her, telling her she didn't need to do it, that he wanted buy her lunch and then sat with her. He was the 'father' she needed at that point-in-time time.

The lyrics of a song say, 'Teach Your Children, Well'. As a father or parent those are wonderful words but not always easy to follow. Parents should, at an early age, teach their children responsibility, respect and truthfulness and discipline.

Throughout my years, I have been blessed by those I have met in life. At the early age of 9, having a paper route and delivering over 150 papers each day at 6am; having to plan the route, collect each week regardless of the weather taught me to deal with the public, manage the money and how to handle those who didn't have the money on the Saturday collection. Sometimes it was begging but later became a matter of grace and forgiving those who didn't pay, because it came out of my own pocket.

I learned I could make more money if I sold more papers, so I convinced my brother he could make some money by helping as well. Later, instead of walking with those big sacks of papers, we bought an old bicycle and wagon. Of course, he rode as I peddled and soon other kids decided to join us. Some from the 'other side' of the tracks; inner city kids whom we didn't like much; then the refugee kids from Hungary who used to chase us. Eventually we all became friends, bought a basketball hoop and nailed it to our garage. It became the gathering place for all of us. We had fun and in a little more than a year our group of poor misfits had the entire business and residential areas as customers. Why do I say blessed? After more than sixty-years, we are still friends and periodically laugh at our exploits.

Did I say, blessed? Yes, by the black mechanic who worked next to our house. He could make a basket from the back-parking lot of the dealership, when no one was looking and make it through the hoop with no net. I don't care what they say, I still think he was LeBron James' father. He also gave me my first Harley Davidson ride and taught me how important it is was to keep your eyes on the road and the car in front.

Since we were in the small town of Barberton, the traffic moved slowly from light to light but that didn't prevent him from glancing to the sidewalk to observe a pretty young blond walking down the street. Well after he explained to the driver whose car he had hit, causing no damage, that he was looking at that young lady, that driver said, "Oh that's ok I was looking at her too." Humility,

106

humor, forgiveness and grace are things we sometimes learn by accident and by experience. These were great learning tools for one so young. So I didn't get my Harley till I was much older and I didn't start looking at blonds until I began going to Sam's Club, but that's another story of being blessed.

Blessed, once again at an early age, to have been hired by a group of family men, comprised of Gentiles and Jews, working together to grow their store operations. Their mentoring, teachings and the responsibility led eventually to becoming the manager of operations and later the opening of a new store.

Throughout our lives we encounter individuals who have an influence on our lives. Our teachers, coaches, school administrators and school personnel all of whom I thought dearly of and respected.

I have to admit, I was not the straight A student I could have been. Maybe I had ADH, most likely it was trying to be somewhere and everywhere at the same time. So my accomplishments in track, football, tennis and swimming seemed to take precedent over French, History and Biology. As you will see, that subject turned out to be very eventful.

Well, I'm blessed to have known a great group of teachers, friends and coaches who gave me the inspiration to get involved with people. I was selected by the teaching staff for the school's Citizenship Award two years in a row, promoting community service work in schools. To this day I cherish and respect the words which appeared on the award. TRUTH, HONOR and INTEGRITY; three words that laid a foundation for a life in business, law enforcement and community service.

It was also the students whom I cherished as friends who throughout my life, remained friends. It was the students who elected me to three years of Student Council, three years to Future Teachers of America and to Junior & Senior Class President.

As mentioned, the school's coaches were always a great inspiration as well. One coach gave me a book titled, "Stand Tall and Straight" by Cleveland Browns tight end, Rev. Bill Glass. It was written with Stan Mosier and Dr. Leslie E. Moser, and advised young men on the use of successful life skills. Rev. Glass, who also worked with Rev. Billy Graham was also inspired to follow a career in ministry.

I remember one chapter dealing with, the 'pollution of mind and body' through the use of drugs and pornography. It was a chapter in which I committed to follow throughout life. Not partaking in the drug du-jour or indulging in various forms of pornography.

Several editions of the book have been printed since the original and I had to purchase one on the aftermarket listing because I gave my original to a young man whom I saw as going down the wrong path in life. But I will always appreciate the thoughtfulness of my coach for it was with his blessing and grace he wished me well in life.

The first week of my senior school year, I went to the office of the school's superintendent, whom I knew well, to tell him I had gotten married during the summer. He graciously said, he appreciated my coming to see him, privately and was there anything he could do. I told him I didn't feel a married student should hold any positions as an officer in the class and new elections needed to take place. He concurred but said it showed the maturity beyond 17 years old. In his typical mild manner, he asked where we were going to live and when I told him, he looked at me and said, I'm so sorry Paul, but you are no longer living in our school district. You will have to attend another school.

Of course, I was devastated but I shook his hand, thanked him and began my walk to the main campus, crying all the way. However, once again I was shown grace, compassion and respect by a man I respected for years. I visited him several times over the years and he would remind me of that day in his office. I told him, maybe had I studied Biology more intensely, I might not have confused it with Greek History when they were talking about, 'Trojans'.

Well, life is good; it's what you make of it. Success comes in many forms; happiness and love may come but once but there is always the future. A future filled with His light and grace, "Lord I want to know you."

About Paul Dimetroff

Mr. Dimtroff is a member of Christ Church at Grove Farm, Sewickley, Pennsylvania www.ccgf.org where he and his wife serve the Savior. The Dimtroffs are engaged in building the Kingdom of God in many ways.

Paul spent over four decades working in corporate and privately held businesses holding positions in Manufacturing, Administration and Marketing. Mr. Dimtroff has served the community in a variety of positions.

- County President of Foster Parent Association
- Vice-Chair to School Board's drug interdiction and busing programs.
- Selected to State Attorneys General Law Enforcement Training Program
- Member of 25-member advisory board to president of major U.S. steel company
- Held positions in Accounting, Administration, H.R., Purchasing and Marketing

Paul and his wife were involved in foster parenting. Over a period of several years, they with their own two young children assisted and helped in raising fifteen other children, ranging in age from a few weeks old to teenagers.

Mr. Dimtroff also became president of a county's Foster Parents Association and worked with the county's Children Services Board, various organizations and state politicians to overturn a state law forbidding the adoption of Foster children by their foster parents. Once the law was passed, his family was the second, in the state of Ohio, to adopt their foster child.

The Dimtroffs were made aware by their teenage foster child, of the ever growing drug problem in high schools. Paul began working with the local school board, CYS and other agencies to determine if and how it could be stopped or controlled. He worked with the African-American community and became Vice Chair to the school board's Advisory Committee on busing and drug interdiction.

To obtain a better understanding of the local drug problem and at the recommendation of a school board member and Director of CYS, Paul applied for and was accepted by the State Attorney General's Law Enforcement Training program.

Paul Dimtroff is on Facebook and can be reached at his email address. Paul would welcome sharing his faith with you!

https://www.facebook.com/paul.dimtroff | pgdsailor@aol.com

Godly Men
Make Godly
Fathers

Never Too Late

By Trevor N. Olsen

Have I been a good father? Sure, and at the risk of sounding a little too overconfident, I can probably say I've done a good job with the 'regular' dad stuff – being there for them, helping, teaching, encouraging, and loving them. Hopefully my kids agree!

But have I been a good Christian father? That's a much tougher question, and I'm afraid I've not done nearly as well in that arena. During my kids most formative years, I'd say I missed the boat on many of my duties as the spiritual head of the household. While I thought I was doing the important 'Dad stuff', I was actually completely ignoring the most important development area for any child – and that is their introduction to Jesus Christ. How is it that we can spend so much time teaching them how to shoot a basketball and learn their multiplication tables, but don't mention anything about what Jesus did for us?

After all, what do I want my kids to remember me for – that I coached their teams when they were little? That I taught them how to ride a bike and use power tools? That I showed them how to be a loving husband to their mother? All those things are good – but there is really only one thing that has any eternal consequence. And that is – did I share Jesus with them? Our kids today are bombarded with a whole lot of noise that is intentionally designed to distract them and us from the one thing we're supposed to be focused on. Don't rely on one hour a week at church to give it to them. Our kids need to learn about Jesus at home. We need to make sure that happens, and the good news is it's never too late to start!

I wish I had a more exciting story to tell about my own Christian faith or a dramatic 'born again' moment that saved me and my family - but there isn't one. Maybe that's what makes it special, at least for me anyway. I'm honored to share my story with you.

Growing Up

I grew up in Cleveland, Ohio as the youngest of four children. I have three older sisters who claim that I was spoiled rotten as we were growing up, although I don't exactly remember it that way.

My parents both came from Christian families and were faithful members of a local church while raising their kids. My mom taught Sunday school and my dad served as an elder of the church. My two oldest sisters made their 8th grade confirmations, but my youngest sister and I never did. By the time we were old enough our parents decided they weren't learning much and they didn't have to prove their faith by sitting in church on Sunday mornings anymore. My mom said we were 'backsliders', but I had no idea what that meant. So my most vivid memories of Sunday mornings were playing tennis or racquetball with the family, and then going out for Sunday brunch. My dad would always order a root beer float before his meal, and he said it tasted great after a good workout.

So I certainly can't attribute the faith that I have today to what I learned in church, since we hardly ever went while I was growing up, other than the obligatory Christmas and Easter services. I recently learned the term "Creasters" – people who only go to church on Christmas and Easter – that's what we were! I'm happy to be an example that just because you didn't go to church much while growing up doesn't mean you can't develop a strong faith later in life. God is very faithful with his people – amen to that!

My dad had a strong quiet faith – which means he didn't talk about it much. So while I didn't learn a lot of biblical history or theological truths from my dad, he did impart on his kids a strong work ethic and devotion to his family. Straight laced and very dependable, his favorite week of the year was the annual family vacation to a resort in Canada. I understand now what a big expense that was for the family budget, but we never missed a year, and we have many great memories and life lessons from those trips. Dad went to heaven on August 14, 2012 – one day after his 80th birthday. I miss him greatly, and I look forward to seeing him again someday. His four kids took his ashes for one last trip down memory lane to that beautiful Canadian resort the year after he went to heaven.

I give my Mom the credit for sharing Jesus with me. Even though she was a self-professed 'backslider', she is actually a very devoted Christian. I can remember a Sunday night when I was about 8 years old - my mom tucked me into bed and she said I should say a prayer to God and to thank Jesus for dying for us. While I don't recall the specifics of my prayer, I do vividly remember an incredible and unexplainable feeling of joy and lightness in my heart. I'm sure I fell asleep a few minutes later and probably forgot about it the next morning and for many years later. I can't explain why I have a lingering memory of that moment some 40 years later, but because I do, I think that was the day I was saved, and I give my mom the credit. Thanks Mom, I love you.

Young adult years

I am sorry to admit that there is a significant portion of my life that I didn't think about God much. Through high school and college and most of my 20's – God was not a part of my life. Why He continued to pursue me through those years when I was ignoring Him, I'll never know - but I am eternally grateful to God for being so patient with me. I know I didn't deserve it.

My wife Chris was raised in a strong Catholic family but had also stopped going to church before we met, so neither one of us had a lot of church in us, but at least we knew we wanted to get married in a church. So we went 'church shopping' and found a nice church in our neighborhood. We got married there in 1994 and had our kids baptized there in 1995 and 1996 shortly after they were born. You might be thinking 'Ok, good start…', but I'd still say we did not have much God in our lives. I don't think we were much more than 'Creasters' for those early years. And then, when our kids were old enough to get involved in sports many of their activities were on Sunday mornings – imagine that. So of course we couldn't deprive our children of the opportunity to participate in those events, so we pretty much stopped going to church. I'm sorry to even say those words now but it gives me a renewed sense of awe at the grace of our loving Father, and even though I continued to turn my back on Him, He never left me. And he hasn't left you either. Amen to that.

Starting a faith journey

We did have a few "religious" habits that carried over into our adult lives. Chris always liked to watch 'The Ten Commandments' on Palm Sunday when it was traditionally shown on TV. I remember watching it with her and we had to ask ourselves who came first – Moses or Jesus - that was the extent of our ignorance of the Bible. It was around that time that I had a thought that I should read the Bible to find out what's in it (I'm sure that was a divinely inspired thought!). So I mentioned to Chris that

I had a new 'bucket list' item to someday read the Bible. Thank the Lord for my good wife, because that year for Christmas she bought me a Bible – the greatest gift I've ever gotten.

It's one thing to have a bible and another thing to actually read it. I don't recall how long it took me to start reading it but I eventually did. And I started at the beginning – "In the beginning, God created..." are the first riveting words of the Bible. I can't say that I was 'all in' from the get go, and I'm sure I went through long spans without reading it at all, but something kept drawing me back. I was interested in the beginning and the end books of the Bible, so I bought an additional study guide on the book of Genesis, which really peaked my interest. And the last book of the bible, Revelation, is so difficult to understand but then I found the "Left Behind" series that tells a riveting fictional story that is easy and entertaining to read. I read through that series of books very quickly, and they have moved around to many members of our extended family as well. I know there are different ways to interpret the end times, and I have no idea if the Left Behind series has the right theology, but I do remember reading it with the mindset of 'This is a possible way things could end.' and really sparking my interest to read more of the Bible. So I eventually read through the entire Bible, and when I got to the end, I started over again. I was becoming more and more enthusiastic about getting some Bible reading time every day.

Then one day I started a journal. I have no idea what prompted me to do that and I don't recall anyone ever suggesting it to me. I was just becoming so moved by some of the verses that I was reading that I felt compelled to start writing them down. My first entry was on September 6, 2007 and it was 2 Corinthians chapter 4 verses 16 - 18

"Therefore we do not lose heart. Though outwardly we are wasting away, yet inwardly we are being renewed day by day. For our light and momentary troubles are achieving for us an eternal glory that far outweighs them all. So we fix our eyes not on what is seen, but on what is unseen. For what is seen is temporary, but what is unseen is eternal."

Powerful words that had a big effect on me. From that point on I began trying to focus my life more on the eternal issues that are unseen, and less on the short term issues of the moment. And I've been writing in a journal ever since, almost 10 years later. As I get older I find myself yearning for more and more of His Word, and rarely does a day go by that I don't start with at least 30-45 minutes of quiet time with just me and His Book. It's the best part of my day.

Work Life

I spent my first 23 years after college working for a large private company. It was a great place to work and I learned a lot about business, although never once was God ever mentioned at work. It was as if it was inappropriate to mix God with professional work life.

Now, I'm mature enough to know that is completely untrue. You can't uncouple your faith from any other part of your life. Your faith is your life. I am so very grateful now that I am a small business owner and I've had the opportunity to join the C12 Group, which is for Christian business owners building great businesses for a greater purpose.

I am so inspired by the people in that C12 Group who are so confident and grounded in their faith that they can wear it on their sleeves and not be shy or embarrassed about sharing their faith. Also, it is what motivates everything they do in every aspect of their lives. That's what I want to get to. So now, at my business we have Bible study every Monday morning. Now, in our mission statement, we boldly proclaim is to "Seek and honor Jesus Christ in everything we do". Now I can't imagine going to work with any other mindset.

Looking Back

For the first 30 years of my life I was a 'Dormant Christian' – I knew something about my faith but didn't think much about it. Then in the last 10 years I've progressed into what I'd call a 'Closet Christian' – building a strong private faith but not sharing it very much. I'm trying to graduate into the next phase of 'Confident Christian', unashamed and unafraid to share my faith to anyone I come in contact with – and of course always with humility and grace and love. I feel like the journey I've been on the last 10 years has me on step 2 of an infinite stairway to Heaven. I can't wait to keep learning and keep climbing those stairs – one at a time!

With both of our kids away at college now, most of our 'at home' time with them is already gone and we can't get that time back. I so wish that they had seen a good example of a Confident Christian Father, and I'm sorry that my journey has been so slow – definitely my own fault, but the good news is it's never too late!

What's Your Ministry?

Shortly before my Dad died, my sister and I were visiting him in the hospital. After seeing all the doctors doing a great job helping my dad, I commented that if I had my career to do over again I would have become a doctor, because I liked the idea of being able to help people get better. My dad said out of the blue "I always thought you should have been a minister." Now, this was the very first time I had ever heard that, and this coming from the father who hardly ever talked about his faith, was now pronouncing on his death bed that he thought his 45-year-old son should have become a minister. My sister laughed out loud and said "Dad, that might have been a good thing to mention 30 years ago".

In hindsight, that was one of the most profound things my Dad ever said to me. Because the truth of the matter is that we are all ministers - not just the guys who work on Sunday mornings. And you don't have to go on overseas mission trips in order to minister to people. Where is your mission field? It's right under your feet. It's with all the people who are around you and that you can touch right where you're at – at work, in your neighborhood, with your friends, and most importantly – at home.

As fathers, we should remember that the single most important job we have here on earth is to minister to our family. Are our words and actions helping to lead our kids toward Christ, or away from Him? This is not meant to cause a guilt trip, and I would be the first in line to confess my guilt over missed opportunities and less-than-perfect role modeling. But no matter where we've come from or how badly we've screwed up in the past, the only thing that matters to God is what we do today and tomorrow, the next day, to start turning ourselves and our families toward Him, instead of away from Him.

The Bible says that the man is to be the spiritual head of the household. So the most important question a man can ask himself is, how am I doing at that job? But don't worry, it's not as intimidating as it sounds - it doesn't mean you have to memorize Bible verses, or interpret scripture, or be able to read the New Testament in the original Greek language.

Being the spiritual head of the household simply means that we are to love our family as Jesus loves us. That means less selfishness, and more service and sacrifice for them, like Jesus did for us. It means loving them unconditionally, and forgiving them when they screw up. It means talking to God about our family and praying for their spiritual and physical well-being. And most importantly, it means not being afraid to talk to our families about God and even praying with them.

Early on in my Christian journey the thought of saying grace at mealtime was a terrifying proposition. The typical fears ran through my head: I don't know how to pray, what would I say? What if I prayed something dumb? What would people think of us if they overheard or saw us praying? Eventually we worked up enough courage as a family to start saying the Lord's Prayer before dinner, and that's all we did for years. Then we had a few other simple prayers that we memorized and it became a little family game to see who could learn and remember them first, and we'd take turns picking which one we wanted to say. Eventually and very gradually we started saying personal prayers, which is a wonderful way to share what's on your heart with your family and God at the same time. What a great way to start a meal and every day!

Being the spiritual head of the household is a role that all fathers should embrace. It shouldn't be a burden or a chore, or something that is too intimidating to try. It's something even the newest Christian father can do – no matter how much we've screwed up in the past, and even if we don't know the first thing about the bible yet. It's a journey that can start today. Our Heavenly Father is ready and waiting to help us! Amen.

About Trevor N. Olsen

Trevor and his wife, Chris, have been married 23 years, living in Frankfort, Illinois and are the proud parents of two college kids – Austin and Bailey. Although their childrearing days are mostly behind them, the job of parenting is never done. They greatly enjoy the time when the kids are home, and they also like being empty-nesters too!

Trevor received a BSME from Rose-Hulman in 1990 and an MBA from Purdue University in 2000. Trevor enjoyed a very successful 23 year corporate career at Panduit Corp, working in and leading engineering, product management, and operations teams.

In 2013, God had a new plan for Trevor and he was guided down a divinely inspired path to the purchase of a small business in Mokena, Illinois – Specialty Plastic Fabricators. Being new to business ownership, Trevor joined the C12 Group, which is composed of Christian business owners "Building Great Businesses for a Greater Purpose". It was from the experience with this group that Trevor has begun his journey from 'closet Christian' to 'confident Christian', and he and his team at work are determined to be good stewards of God's business for the glory of His Son Jesus Christ. For the past two years they have started the work week with the highest priority - Bible Study, which is the foundation of their business and lives.

Trevor is an avid reader and eager to become a better husband, a better father, and most importantly, a faithful follower of Jesus Christ

Email: trevor@spfinc.com

Facebook: https://www.facebook.com/trevor.olsen.37625

LinkedIn: https://www.linkedin.com/in/trevor-olsen-929a3b31/

Company websites: www.spfinc.com

www.fastenersplusintl.com

Fathering 101

By Darcy Hawk

Your children are not your children;

They are the sons and daughters of

Life's longing for itself.

They come through you

but they are not from you

And though they are with you

They belong not to you.

Sweet Honey In the Rock

On October 21st 1976 my wife brought a little astronaut into the universe. The nurse handed her over to me immediately after launch like Cape Canaveral hands the mission over to the Johnson Space Center.

Who in their right mind could expect my wife and me to prepare this little human to boldly go, (split infinitives are now OK? I did not see that coming wow!), where none have gone before? How does NASA prepare someone for space/time travel? They consult experts who have studied space flight and human physiology.

Looking around the only experienced child raisers were the ones who messed us up. Would my remote father and deceased mother be much help? What about the in-laws? They seemed to do a half decent job raising my wife but one of them was insisting my daughter needed a belly band to make sure she had an innie on her tummy.

Lord of mercy, such things were actually available at the five and dime. Well, she was launched and in orbit so every source of support was needed to keep her on track and in flight.

If things work as hoped I will be a pile of ashes while she journeys on to see and know things that are unimaginable to me. After all since my father died in 1979 I have seen and encountered things that were impossible for him to predict.

So what did he give me for the journey? And what did the crazy old tobacco spitting man who raised him give my father? Once I tried the line, "Well that's what my parents did to me." on my wife. She said, "That doesn't mean it was right."

True, some of what I got was garbage and some of what I gave was garbage, but sorting through it all helps me to fasten on the riches. One insight was distance from dad hints at similarities to dad. If I found it hard to talk and share it was because he found it hard to talk and share. So, perhaps imagining what would cause me to behave in a certain way might just give me insight into my daughter.

It also helps to realize the things you hate about your kids are there because you put them there and may be they are things you hate about yourself. Of course without fact checking this all amounts to speculation because our children are like us but they are not us. Always like me, but different, she defies comfortable assumptions and keeps her mystery.

After the initial lift off like a multi stage rocket came many succeeding newly developed people, and it was hard to keep up.

126

Presents from distant relatives tell the tale – a too small hand crocheted sweater in a bunny pattern can be "sooo last year".

Each edition of my daughter seemed to last forever, like the one who took hours to fall asleep, the one who played *Christmas With Barbie* over and over, and the one who plastered magazine photos of Danny, Donny, Joe, John; Jordan over her bedroom walls.

> Nothing I cared, in the lamb white days,
> that time would take me...
>
> Up to the swallow thronged loft by the shadow of my hand,
> In the moon that is always rising,
> Nor that riding to sleep
> I should hear him fly with the high fields
> And wake to the farm forever fled from the childless land.
> Oh as I was young and easy in the mercy of his means,
> Time held me green and dying
> Though I sang in my chains like the sea.

From *Fern Hill* by Dylan Thomas

Our own childhood is not observed by us, it is lived and observed by others. I know the fleeting moments that flowed into the woman my daughter has become. Sometimes the wisdom of my parents supplied responses and answers that worked for her as they worked for me but they could not see the world of now.

Part of the job is not to get in the way of what evolution has provided because we come from a long line of travelers who went to undiscovered countries and lived long enough to make our ancestors. Fathering is never done alone. It isn't even reliant on the people living and breathing at the time.

Standing in the medieval hostel in Canterbury England I had a strong sense that some among my ancestors who stopped there

127

while making the pilgrimage from London to the tomb of Thomas Becket in Chaucer's time. They were parents who raised children who eventually produced the parents who raised me. Some father's actions a thousand years ago came down along with the DNA to subtly inform how I relate to my daughter.

We are all supplied with families and communities to help and teach, but humans also have onboard computers preprogrammed with operating systems. Children teach as well as learn and they help teach us how to care for them. My daughter was not a Miranda created by me but someone being formed from within. She expressed opinions and preferences that worked in her world from early on.

Who doesn't like ice cream? What person prefers dill pickles to sweet pickles? What strange being prefers fish sticks over chocolate cake? This means Fathers do not build children. I didn't have to build a child, I had to guide a child.

But I like designing and building things. Measuring, cutting, joining, sanding, varnishing and voila she is complete. Most men have to make an effort not to fix, not to remodel, not to reach for the tool box. After all to a man with a hammer all the world is a nail. Judgement, observation and patience are important when preparing someone to meet the unexpected.

If you can't avoid being Mr. Fixit make sure your parenting tools are Swiss Army style. Prepare to be versatile and have the confidence to test your brilliant idea with others, try and err while sharing fun in learning. Kids are amazingly self-correcting with a God given gyroscope. They can be bent with consistently bad parenting but imperfect parenting is normal and most of our children turn out normal, at least within acceptable standard deviations from the mean.

About The Rev. Dr. Darcy Hawk

Darcy can be reached through Facebook and his email.

Darcy Hawk djhawk@zoominternet.net

https://www.facebook.com/darcy.hawk

Godly Men
Make Godly
Fathers

Fatherhood Basics, Your Wife Reflects The Quality of Your Fatherhood

By Ron Razete

Love and affection towards your wife, that is the foundation to the family.

The foundation of any family is built upon the love that men have for their wives and of course the love that wives have for their husbands. Although this may seem rudimentary, it is never-the-less vital to any positive parenting. You and your spouse have a brand of sorts... a love brand that communicates an inward message towards each other and an outward message to the world.

This includes every form of communication whether intended or unintended. Words, facial expressions, body language, tone of voice and even silence are woven together in a tapestry of affection or disdain, warmth or chilled, open or hidden.

Children will always see their world through the prism of their parents' love affair. The strength and beauty of that relationship, its gravitas and its perceived permanence and visible power to overcome adversity, are an all-important backdrop to what is understood and learned by your children.

The job of raising kids is challenging enough without adding inherent vice to the delivery of love, care and instruction. Remember… you are always witnessing in essence (to use a Christian term) or giving "testimony" to what you believe. Saying one thing and behaving in a contradictory way will not be lost on your kids (or your spouse).

They will discount your direction with their actions and eventually with their words, if you are substantially inconsistent in your message. If we were talking about training a family dog for example, this would be obvious. But somehow, we often forget that this is true in every area of life! Especially for our parenting.

Being an effective father has much to do with delivering the right message at the right time. Initially the message is "be careful", "repeat after me", "do this" and "don't do that", "look both ways before crossing the street" and etcetera.

Of course, fatherhood is much more than just a series of messages, but broken down to the base level, actions and words are the delivery of some message... whether intended or unintended. What is your marriage brand message? The most vital message of all is that, as a father, you chose this woman from all the women on earth and that you love her with an unconditional love.

This brand message, although rarely communicated well, is the only foundation for the long term, God pleasing, glorifying "agape" love. Not an empty slogan or advertisement, but for many men the most difficult thing is to love their wives in a vibrant, visible and consistent way. In other words, one of the keys to effective, positive parenting is having a marriage that is awesome and contagious.

Having five adult children (three of them married) and also having conversations about the challenges and benefits of marriage has been illuminating. I've been affirmed in my suspicion that one of the most important aspects of raising my children was in fact putting my love for their mother on display. All of my family members have witnessed first-hand the ups and downs, ins and outs of a forever love.

You may be saying, "I'm just not that kind of man" or "my wife doesn't like that gushy, type of love". Although that may be accurate, your "dad brand" doesn't have to be stuck. It can evolve toward the best balance for your entire parenting platform. I'm advocating some movement toward a more obvious and visible expression of love for your wife.

All brands require refocusing and redirection. I'm not just talking about what you say to one another in private, although every man should affirm his love for his wife sincerely, often and with passion. But, if you want to really parent from a position of strength, it will take every kind of "love language" expression imaginable.

As the father of five (now adults), I can vouch for this!

Sadly, this world is not a fan of the biblical marriage model. In fact, men have discarded their role in the family and the result has been a culture adrift and openly hostile to the traditional family and certainly the traditions of male and female roles in the family. It has discarded and mocked God (read Romans 1 18-32), while attempting to prove to the world that no standards, morals or folkways are needed.

You can make every relationship up as you go along! Of course, the result of this assault on traditional biblical values and marriage roles has torn our culture apart in very measurable ways. I could quote statistics, but it is so bad and so obvious, I won't waste your time. If you are reading this book, you already sense the need for some help and coaching if you want to have a loving, strong family that will stand the test of time.

If your "brand' of marriage and family is not built solidly on the timeless truths found in the Bible, you are being tragically misguided.

Here, I will resist the temptation to give you a "how to" guide to loving your wife. That isn't where you should start. Instead, I'm going to call you to start with prayer. And then some more prayer. Followed by more prayer until you begin to feel the way you did when you were madly in love with your wife. That could have been as recently as this morning or so long ago that you laugh at the suggestion that you can do something to reverse the often natural distance and degradation of affection that is all too commonplace in marriages.

If there HAS been some distance or degradation in your love affair, prayer can and will begin to put things right. Focusing on your most basic purpose; to know God more and more and to glorify him with your whole self... you begin to rediscover the treasure that is your wife.

The next suggestions will hopefully give you some tools to reach greater and greater heights of love and affection with your Mrs., your spouse.

Since my wife and I are more spontaneous as a couple than most, you may either want to move more in a different direction (slowly at first to make sure your wife doesn't think you are crazy) and begin to get excited about some new adventures.

Change things up!

New challenges are encouraged. For example, my wife and I decided to hike the Grand Canyon from Rim to Rim in a single day on our 33rd wedding anniversary!

How's that for an adventure? We've never hiked much in the past, but the more we talked about the idea (her idea actually) the more we agreed that it would be very hard but very exciting at the same time. Since my wife and I work in different careers, we had to take extra time to meet this new challenge.

This trip to the Canyon required 3 months of planning and preparation. We walked together and did some practice hikes. We also worked out our meals and our hydration plan, etc. It was very fun and it drew us together in ways we didn't know were undeveloped.

We would have both said that our love affair was about as good as it could get, but now we both acknowledge that we have reached new heights. In fact, we are already going back to the Canyon to hike it again, and take our adult children with us to experience the majesty of God's creation together. It's not the Grand Canyon that we credit for our new-found intimacy, rather the Creator and His Grace and Mercy.

Once you begin to grow again in your affection, the physical aspect of your relationship will also be reinvigorated. And although my children, at reading this, will all be pretending to put their fingers down their throats in a mock attempts to vomit, it is obvious to them what my wife and I think and feel about one another. It is as clear to them as the way we worship God and seek to glorify Him in all things.

I can assure you that "do as I say and not as I do" doesn't work with raising children OR loving your wife. The husband and father must lead. Yes, it IS your responsibility to love your wife even when she isn't returning that love. Leading is putting down your needs and embracing your wife, your family and those that God leads you to care for.

Now, that idea might seem counter-intuitive but I assure you that it is one of the great truths of life. Loving someone always changes everything. It changes the way we feel, the way others see us and the way we cooperate with God as He weaves our lives together in a way that brings Him glory.

Books that suggest that you do this or that and make your wife think you are now really trying, are not helpful in the long run. Lists of things that you didn't think up yourself are just that… lists.

When you return to your less affectionate self, your wife will only be more jaded now than ever. She will feel silly, believing that you are REALLY changing. That's why real change is required and prayer is the foundation of that change.

Your prayers might just spark a desire to shake up a number of areas in your life that have long needed attention. Your waistline for example… or your finances… or your family relationships. Prayer can and will move you forward in all areas of your life. I needed to lead in the area of fitness and I wasn't leading at all. Instead, I was using food as a pleasure substitute rather than my marriage being the source of that enjoyment. Although we were often together eating out at nicer and nicer restaurants, we were not feeling great about ourselves or our time together when we returned home.

We both decided to embark on somewhat of a "total body makeover". Hiking and changing our eating habits not only helped us go 24 miles in one day, it harnessed and redirected all of the energy and resources that we used to focus on eating out and relaxing.

The results are awesome!

You may be thinking that prayer is not your strong-suit... I am right there with you. I am adequate when it comes to praying as requested for others, for our children's safety, for their health and for aches and pains, but I was not very adequate at all when praying that God would change ME.

Now, I see that I should have started with the "God change ME prayers" long ago. I now understand that my Heavenly Father wants to spend time with me, to hear from me and to continue the work in me that God started in 1981 when I first yielded to Him in prayer by giving him my very life. It is THAT work that he wants to continue, and it goes much smoother when I am asking for His input and direction and believing that He will bring everything to pass that He promises.

Loving your wife isn't the only thing that is required to be a great father, but it is PRIMARY and VITAL.

In the best families, you will find at the center a couple that is deeply, obviously and affectionately in love.

About Ron Razete

Former youth director and now founder of Peace, Love and Little Donuts, Ron and his wife Marci are calling the metropolis of Pittsburgh, Pennsylvania their home base. You can reach Ron at ronrazete@mac.com

Your Call To Action

In this book you have read wonderfully written, inspirational stories! You are now a part of our lives, I mean existentially. Your existence and ours are now intertwined for however long you remember anything in this book.

Please respond to what you have read in at least one (1) of the following calls to respond, okay?

1. Let the author know how his chapter impacted you. You can use the contact information for that author found at the end of his chapter.
2. Please let Motivation Champs Publishing know that in your opinion, Motivation Champs Publishing did a GREAT JOB with this work.
3. Here it is, please, ACCEPT JESUS CHRIST AS YOUR LORD AND SAVIOR! This will, guaranteed, make the most AWESOME and permanent positive change in your life, now and for eternity!
4. Go to Amazon.com and make a review of our work, our book, Godly Men Make Godly Fathers.

Thank you for reading and for your interest; I personally thank you for this! Really, it makes a difference. It's not easy to write and to put oneself out there... I'm sure you get that. GOD BLESS YOU AND KEEP YOU, beloved reader! ☺   Doug Lauffer

Godly Men
Make Godly
Fathers

Great Books for Fathers

This is a very short list of great Christian book that are guaranteed to inspire you.

1. *The Hiding Place* by Corrie ten Boom
2. *Through Gates of Splendor* by Elisabeth Elliot
3. *God's Smuggler* by Brother Andrew
4. *In Search of Certainty* by John Guest
5. *Surprised by Joy: The Shape of My Early Life* by C.S. Lewis
6. *Tortured for Christ* by Richard Wurmbrand
7. *The Confessions of St. Augustine* by Augustine of Hippo
8. *No Compromise* by Melody Green
9. *Hudson Taylor's Spiritual Secret* by Howard Taylor
10. *Bonhoeffer: Pastor, Martyr, Prophet, Spy* by Eric Metaxas
11. *PRAY, A Study for Men and Boys* by Doug Lauffer
12. *The Cross and the Switchblade* by David Wilkerson
13. *Rees Howells: Intercessor* by Norman P. Grubb
14. *In My Father's House* by Corrie ten Boom
15. *Run Baby Run* by Nicky Cruz
16. *UP: Getting UP is the Key to Life* by Brian P. Swift
17. *Taking Back The Rainbow* by Mark Pudlowski

Helpful Resources for You and Your Children on Social Media

https://www.internetmatters.org/advice/social-media/

https://www.aap.org/en-us/advocacy-and-policy/aap-health-initiatives/Pages/Media-and-Children.aspx

https://www.promotionworld.com/se/articles/article/170818-only-backschool-social-media-resources-you-will-ever-need

For finding more on this topic every month, use the following phrase as a search string of words in a web search engine like Bing or Google.

More Helpful Resources for You and Your Children on Social Media

Godly Men
Make Godly
Fathers

A Treasury of Scripture Passages

Encouragement from God's Word for Any Situation
(Passages come from the King James Version of The Holy Bible.)

2 Timothy 1:7 - *For God hath not given us the spirit of fear; but of power, and of love, and of a sound mind.*

Psalms 37:4 - *Delight thyself also in the LORD; and he shall give thee the desires of thine heart.*

Psalms 121:1-8 - (A Song of degrees.) *I will lift up mine eyes unto the hills, from whence cometh my help.*

Proverbs 30:5 - *Every word of God [is] pure: he [is] a shield unto them that put their trust in Him.*

Mark 11:24 - *Therefore I say unto you, what things whatsoever ye desire, when ye pray, believe that ye receive, and ye shall have.*

Psalms 28:7 - *The LORD [is] my strength and my shield; my heart trusted in him, and I am helped: therefore my heart greatly rejoices; and with my song will I praise Him.*

Psalms 34:4 - *I sought the LORD, and he heard me, and delivered me from all my fears.*

Philippians 4:13 - *I can do all things through Christ who strengthens me.*

1 Thessalonians 5:9-11 - *For God hath not appointed us to wrath, but to obtain salvation by our Lord Jesus Christ,* (Read More...)

Psalms 55:22 - *Cast thy burden upon the LORD, and He shall sustain thee: He shall never suffer the righteous to be moved.*

145

Jeremiah 29:11 - *For I know the thoughts that I think toward you, says the LORD, thoughts of peace, and not of evil, to give you an expected end.*

Romans 15:13 - *Now the God of hope fill you with all joy and peace in believing, that ye may abound in hope, through the power of the Holy Ghost.*

Psalms 126:5 - *They that sow in tears shall reap in joy.*

Jeremiah 29:11-14 - *For I know the thoughts that I think toward you, says the LORD, thoughts of peace, and not of evil, to give you an expected end.*

John 16:33 - *These things I have spoken unto you, that in me ye might have peace. In the world ye shall have tribulation: but be of good cheer; I have overcome the world.*

Ephesians 4:29 - *Let no corrupt communication proceed out of your mouth, but that which is good to the use of edifying, that it may minister grace unto the hearers.*

Hebrews 10:25 - *Not forsaking the assembling of ourselves together, as the manner of some [is]; but exhorting [one another]: and so much the more, as ye see the day approaching.*

Hebrews 4:12 - *For the word of God [is] quick, and powerful, and sharper than any two-edged sword, piercing even to the dividing asunder of soul and spirit, and of the joints and marrow, and [is] a discerner of the thoughts and intents of the heart.*

John 3:16, 17 - *For God so loved the world, that He gave His only begotten Son, that whosoever believeth in Him should not perish, but have everlasting life. For God sent not His Son into the world to condemn the world; but that the world through Him might be saved.*

Godly Men
Make Godly
Fathers